Update on Christian Counseling

VOLUME TWO

Jay E. Adams

BAKER BOOK HOUSE
Grand Rapids, Michigan 49506

"Does the Behaviorist Have a Mind," by Wm. Hallock Johnson, was first
published in *The Princeton Theological Review*, January, 1927.

PHOTOLITHOPRINTED BY CUSHING - MALLOY, INC.
ANN ARBOR, MICHIGAN, UNITED STATES OF AMERICA

To
my new daughter,
Lucy Anne

Contents

Introduction

Over the past 12 years I have worked assiduously to produce a body of literature in a field that, prior to that time, virtually did not exist: the field of biblical counseling. In some measure, I believe that I have succeeded. But, because important issues crop up from time to time and constantly studies on vital topics must be done, that do not appropriately fit into any given book that is currently being prepared, I began to publish the reports on these in an open-ended series of books entitled, *Update on Christian Counseling,* of which this is the second volume.

In volume II, I treat mostly current miscellaneous matters, as you would expect from the title. But, for the first time, I have also made available a valuable article, from a past era, that has for long been out of print. Though it might seem inappropriate to reprint anything in a volume entitled *Update,* I have discovered that the old is often the newest and most up-to-date of all. Apart from a few dated references, the article is as fresh and timely as if it had just been written.

I consider the study in I Corinthians 13 significant and hope that it will become a useful resource for counseling. Two very recent trends have been considered: (1) extra-biblical guidance, (2) father-images of God, and one that has troubled us for some years: transactional analysis.

Other matters also have been touched upon. All are calculated to help biblical counselors to do a more effective job *today.*

Blessings!
JAY ADAMS
The Millhouse
1981

1
Do Fathers Make Atheists of Their Children?

The other day I received a phone call from a sympathetic, well-meaning pastor who raised a question that I have been hearing increasingly, in one place or another, over the last few years. It was, in substance, this:

> If a child has been raised by a father whose life is a miserable example, won't that child grow up with a wrong conception of God and find it difficult to trust and obey Him, since he will base his ideas of what God is like on his own father's behavior?

This is a very serious question, which—if the assumption on which it is based is true—has widespread implications for counseling as well as for Christian education. The teaching behind the question must be considered and all confusion that is connected with it must be dispelled in the pure light of biblical clarity.

To begin with, I told him, "Of course, all sorts of things are possible. It is altogether possible, therefore (although in all my counseling I have never seen it), that some child, somewhere, because of the sinful perverseness of his adamic nature, has done just what the questioner suggests.[1] If a child does so, obviously he will get an entirely wrong view of God. This will be true whether his earthly father succeeds or fails. (All fail somewhere; and even in their successes there are great limitations.) To learn about God from looking at even the best father is to develop erroneous and sinful concepts of God. All sorts of difficulties in one's relationship to God are bound to crop up as a result."

But, let us look at the question again. It *presupposes* that children grow up

---

1. Perhaps more and more we shall see this occurring if children are taught to learn of God by looking at their fathers (to teach them to do so, naturally, is the logical implication of this strange unbiblical doctrine). The notion is beginning to spread: cf. Bruce Narramore, *Parenting with Love and Limits* (Zondervan: Grand Rapids, 1979), pp. 29, 90ff.

identifying God with their own fathers.[2] Does this really happen? Does it take place in the life of *every* child or even in the life of most—or many? And if so, what does the Bible have to say about this supposedly powerful and most important way of teaching children about God, the heavenly Father? Surely, if this is where children learn their earliest and most basic ideas of God, the Bible must not be silent about it! But, strange to say, that is just the point—the Bible knows nothing, absolutely nothing, about this notion.

Where, then, does the notion come from? Paul Meier, assistant professor of practical theology at Dallas Theological Seminary, writes:

> In psychiatry, we learn that an adult's attitudes toward God are influenced greatly by his attitudes toward his own father while he was growing up.[3]

He tells of a "patient" (notice the medical model) who was a "devout atheist" (a strange combination of words for an evangelical theology professor) and comments: "And I would have expected him to be, given the kind of father image he grew up with." (Notice again the psychological jargon.) Of persons raised in such situations, in general, he says (note, throughout the psychological rather than biblical orientation Meier takes):

> In their subconscious minds [not a biblical construct], they want to believe there is no God because they resent the fact that they had no father, or one who was nearly always absent and negativistic. . . . Some of these patients hated their fathers so much that they became atheists as an unconscious rebellion against the existence of their fathers.[4]

Meier is clear enough about the source of such views. He gets the notion not from the Bible, but from "psychiatry." Of course, he cannot mean *all* psychiatrists. They disagree so greatly among themselves that it is almost

---

2. Imitation of fathers is one thing (and even that is far from inevitable, as Ezek. 18 indicates), but identification of God with one's father is quite another.

3. To indicate by the phrase "In psychiatry, we learn" that there is anything like agreement on the part of most psychiatrists about this—or anything else—indicates either naivete by Meier or (what is more likely) his assumption of naivete on the part of his readers. What is a psychiatrist doing teaching "practical theology"? And from "psychiatry" rather than the Bible?

4 Paul Meier, *Christian Child Rearing and Personality Development* (Grand Rapids: Baker Book House, 1977), pp. 29, 30.

ludicrous to say "psychiatrists think," "psychiatrists teach," "psychiatrists believe," or (as he does) to speak of "psychiatry" as though this were a monolithic science holding to any particular view. From his description of the belief, however, it would seem that he refers to some psychiatrist(s) of a Freudian or neo-Freudian bent.[5] Just whom, he does not say.

Be that as it may, the important thing to see is that the notion that children identify God with their fathers, Meier says, comes not from the Bible, but from an outside (pagan) source. In that, he is correct.

Consistently, Meier finds that good fathers develop in their children "a healthy concept of God," and that, "If they haven't already put their faith in Jesus Christ, they do so readily when I show them God's simple plan of salvation."[6]

It all sounds so simple, so neat and compact! But is it? Is the predisposition of a child to trust Christ as Savior directly linked to his "father image"?[7]

As I have said already, in a rare case or so, possibly this dynamic could occur, without all the Freudian embellishments, of course; but it certainly could not be considered a common thing—surely not a *rule* of personality development, the basic principle of Christian education and the predisposing factor in grace, as Meier makes it—because the Bible never, not even once, makes a point of it! If it is so important in the raising of children to give them their earliest views of God through their earthly fathers that, with Meier, we must say, "I hope those of us who are fathers, or who someday will be fathers, will grasp the heavy responsibility that God has given us,"[8] then why doesn't he show us where, in the Bible, God tells us this is so? We cannot base theological doctrine on "psychiatry"! Has God allowed His church to exist for 1900 years (and the OT church for a longer period prior to that) without this vital information? Did He allow us to go all that time condemning our children to atheism because we did not yet have Freud's (or Meier's) insights? Was our doctrine of salvation defective until Meier told us what to believe about this crucial matter?

---

5. Note the jargon "father image," "subconscious mind," etc.
6. Ibid., p. 31.
7. There is some strange preparationist theology in this notion and an incipient weakening of the doctrine of total depravity.
8. Meier, op. cit., p. 31.

If this idea were really all that important, the God who told us that He had given us "all things that pertain to life and godliness" (II Pet. 1:3) must have said so somewhere. But search the Bible from stem to stern, and you will find neither a hint nor a whisper of this "father image" doctrine that supposedly leads either to atheism or to the ready acceptance of the gospel.

We can only conclude that Meier is wrong in importing into the church (and her doctrine) any such ideas. Sad, that at Dallas seminary, a school that over the years purported to base its teaching on biblical exposition alone, someone now teaches doctrine based on the wild theories of some outmoded psychiatrists! Students who accept such teaching will now go out to place responsibilities (erroneously said to be from God) on the shoulders of the members of their congregations that neither they nor their fathers should have borne! Think of it—admittedly pagan psychiatric dogma taught as Christian doctrine!

Now, of course, I would not want to deny the importance of parental teaching—especially by the father, whom the Bible singles out for such a responsibility (Deut. 8; Eph. 6:1-4; Col. 3:21). Parental influence on a child, by word and by life, is enormous. That is not at issue.

The nub of my argument with Meier's doctrine is this: he lays additional burdens on parents' shoulders that the Bible does not, and he calls these responsibilities God-given. It is one thing to say that one's teaching, by word and life, will be of major significance (but not utterly determinative) to a child's development. It is quite another to say,

1. his salvation or lack of it will depend on whether an earthly father lives like the heavenly Father (who ever did?),
2. that this child's concepts of God will be developed from the father's image,
3. and that the child necessarily will be influenced even into adult life by this image. (Meier tells us about a Ph.D. supposedly affected that way[9] and says those influenced negatively "never really feel forgiven,"[10] etc.)

---

9. Ibid., p. 29.

10. Ibid., p. 30. *Feeling* forgiven is also a nonbiblical construct (cf. my detailed comments on the nature and effects of forgiveness in *More than Redemption: A Theology of Christian Counseling* [Phillipsburg, N.J.: Presbyterian and Reformed, 1979]).

It is *such a construct* of parental responsibility—not parental responsibility itself—against which I must protest.

First, no child will ever grow up with a proper concept of God if he must depend on getting it from his father—even a good father. No father, in any way, even comes close to reflecting the heavenly Father accurately. If what Meier says is true, *all* children are doomed; not just some.

Secondly, Meier has put the cart before the horse (a hallmark of psychiatric thinking). Biblically, the father learns how to be a father by emulating the way that God treats him as His child: "bring them up with the nurture and admonition of the Lord" (Eph. 6:4). That is to say, an earthly father is to discipline his children as God does His. God's fatherhood is the standard against which all others are measured; God, the Father, is the model for all earthly fathers. One does not measure good money against counterfeit; he measures the counterfeit against the good. Never are earthly fathers held forth as the model for children to determine what God is like.

Thirdly, no "father image" could properly teach a child about God's love, justice, omniscience, omnipotence, omnipresence, wrath, mercy, etc. All these truths about God must be learned from the Bible and what it teaches by precept and example. God's love, for instance, is not taught through observing the love of one's father (that may, of course, get a hearing for it), but by pointing a child to the cross (I John 4:10).

Fourthly, fathers are to *teach* their children about God *from the Bible* (Deut. 6, etc.). It is their task to teach all that God revealed in the Scriptures about Himself (Deut. 29:29), pointing not to themselves—except perhaps now and then by contrast—but to the God who has made Himself known in special revelation.

Fifthly, and, as for Ph.D.s (and other adults) who are supposedly stuck with their infantile concepts of God, being adversely influenced all their later life (see Meier's fuller account of this: pp. 30ff.), all one can say is that it is time to teach them to give up childish ways now that they have become adults![11]

Sixthly, it is doubtful, however, that there exists such a widespread influence of fathers on their children's concept of God with such bad effects.

---

11. Strange, that the Corinthians (and others like them) could come to Christ with no such difficulty even though their parents were not Christians but pagans.

(What the Ph.D.'s problem *really* was would be interesting to know.) Meier, like the rest of us, doubtless tends to find what he is looking for. We all come to the counseling room with presuppositions, i.e., views, and viewpoints that grow out of them, that we hold as true, and upon which, therefore, we base other views and actions. These presuppositions, indeed, make us all selective of the data upon which we focus attention, and color our interpretations of them. There is no such thing as uninterpreted "objective" data for any counselor.

A typical, obvious example is Tim LaHaye's viewpoint on temperament. Having once adopted this (admittedly) unbiblical, pagan Greek construct for typing individuals, he sees counselees, Bible characters, people who want their future predicted, etc., in the light of the presuppositions inherent in that dogma. Even the Bible is interpreted in terms of the four temperaments (and combinations thereof). The pigeonholes in the framework are built out of nonbiblical materials; then Bible characters (Paul, Peter), as well as Tom and Suzie counselee, are fitted into the holes their characters seem best to approximate. In this system, the Bible is used to support and illustrate the extra-biblical theory rather than the reverse. If temperament were as big a thing as LaHaye says it is, the Bible would be full of it. But, like Meier (and all others who reverse the proper procedure) the framework of the theory is constructed out of pagan materials (i.e., from unbiblical presuppositions, about man, God, and the universe). We do not have to reach *beyond* the Bible for our presuppositions; they should always be biblical. Only then can we evaluate, judge and control our other beliefs based on them in a way that keeps us on track. Since one's presuppositions determine how he will handle data, it is important for him to be sure that those presuppositions are scriptural. That is the only way to be sure that his presuppositions will not lead him astray.

Take Meier's case. He is off the track scripturally because of his presuppositions. Not only does he presuppose a kind of Freudianism to be true, but he seems to presuppose that, at least at times, God Himself speaks as authoritatively through Freud as through the Bible. What "psychiatry" says is taken as "the heavy responsibility that God has given us" (p. 31). That presupposition itself is perhaps the most dangerous of all. Yet, I am fairly certain that Meier would never articulate it himself as true. Nevertheless,

6

unwittingly, he has adopted a method that grows out of and is appropriate to such a presupposition.

If so important a matter as one's concept of God (surely a central biblical concern if there ever was one) depends on the image of God seen in his father, why is the Bible as silent as it is on the temperament issue? Why does Meier find it necessary to go beyond Scriptures to "psychiatry" for the concept? Here is where so much danger lies. To Meier, LaHaye[12] and others who tend to do so, Paul's warning should serve as a needed corrective:

> Now these things I have applied figuratively to myself and to Apollos for your sakes, brothers, in order that you may learn from us not to go beyond what has been written (I Cor. 4:6, *The NT in Everyday English*).

---

12. On this point. Other things LaHaye teaches are biblical. What makes him become so unbiblical at this point?

2

Liberty with a Limit

(Including a Note on Questionable Sexual Practices)

The problem at Corinth that gave rise to the important discussion of the limits of Christian liberty concerned the matter of eating food sacrificed to pagan idols. After an animal had been dedicated and sacrificed to a heathen god or goddess, it was sold in the meat market at a bargain price because, in effect, it was used, secondhand meat. Many of the early Christians, at Corinth at least (cf. 1:26), were of the poorer classes, and some even were slaves. Quite naturally, it would be advantageous for them to purchase this more reasonably priced meat. But they had broken with paganism, and wanted rightly to avoid all that smacked of pagan worship. Consequently, the question arose, "May Christians eat food that has been sacrificed to idols without participating in idolatry?"

In answering this specific question, Paul lays down a general principle that we must study because of its pertinence to many counseling problems. The counselor will find that a clear perspective on this matter will stand him in good stead when he is required to give biblical direction in cases of conscience.

We shall look at Paul's teaching in order to discover the general principle involved, how it applies to Christian living and its place in counseling.

What did Paul tell the Corinthians?

The question first arises in chapter eight of I Corinthians. Then he takes a detour to touch on other matters, only to return to the subject in chapter 10. As concisely as possible, I shall try to restate Paul's answers to the various inquiries that had been made, as he gives them in these two chapters.

First, Paul sketches the situation, pointing up the major issue. He says all have some knowledge about the matter, but it is possible that some are misinformed (8:1-3). He says, furthermore, that a person who may not be correctly informed may have problems with his conscience because of habits formed when still a participant in an idolatrous religion:

> There are some who, out of habit formed in idolatry, still eat food as if it were offered to an idol, and because their conscience is weak, they are defiled (v. 7b).

Then, he says, the one who has no problem with knowledge or with his own conscience nevertheless may have missed entirely another important issue— his influence upon another brother whose conscience is weak.[1]

Strong Christians (i.e., those with a strong conscience on the matter) realize that there is no harm in eating meat that has been sacrificed to idols, since idols are nothing; there is only one true God (4-6). But "everybody doesn't know this" (7a). The brother who thinks that it is idolatry to eat (or that it *might* be idolatry to do so) is the one with the weak conscience. Therefore, since it is sin for such weak brothers to eat, they are "defiled" (7c) by doing so. The *meat* did not defile them, of course. They were defiled by doing what they thought was or might have been sin. For them, to eat was to slip back into idolatry in their hearts. It is important to be clear about this fact: because the *food* was not contaminated (the weak brother himself is said to be contaminated),[2] some (strong brothers) could eat righteously, but others (weak brothers) could not; if they ate, for them it was sin. In other words, it is a Christian principle that the very same act under conditions stated here can for some be perfectly acceptable, but for others be sin.[3]

But that is not all. While strong brothers have liberty to eat whatever is pure in God's sight, there is a limitation to that liberty. If the brother with the stronger (better informed) conscience pursues a course of life in which he freely enjoys his rights and privileges in a selfish and thoughtless way, his freedom becomes license and he sins. His freedom to partake of food offered

---

1. A conscience is said to be weak when improperly informed. The capacity to make self-evaluation and to trigger peaceful or painful bodily responses is called conscience; it functions in accordance with standards that may or may not be biblical. Weak consciences are those that operate according to faulty, unbiblical values.

2. Cf. Titus 1:15 for a similar comment. Again, the defiling comes from within; not from without.

3. Paul put it well in Romans when he wrote: "Whatever isn't of faith is sin" (Rom. 14:23). There, he says that if one eats doubting, he sins. He must know fully that what he is doing is proper before God or he shouldn't do it at all.

to idols may not be pushed to the point where he becomes a stumbling block in the path of his weaker brother. He must forego his right (v. 9) whenever it becomes the occasion for tempting a weaker brother to sin.

If a brother who doesn't have his knowledge (perhaps a recent, uninstructed convert) should see him eating, this may tempt him to do the same. But, since persons who have a different conscience about the act can do the same thing righteously or sinfully, the stronger brother will have led his weaker brother into sin, and possibly back into idolatry (8:10-13). Thus, the conscience of another cannot be ignored when his acts are influenced by one's own example. No man is an island. Such thoughtlessness is sin—against the weaker brother and against Christ (v. 12).

Again, N.B., it is not the eating, in and of itself, that is sin, but rather the careless or indifferent attitude of the one who eats, heedless of its effect upon others. Here, in no uncertain terms, Paul affirms the truth that a Christian is his brother's keeper! It is, therefore, an unqualified principle that the indifferent practices one has the *right* (v. 9 uses the word) to enjoy become moral issues for him when their exercise becomes a hindrance to the life of another Christian.

The privilege must be abandoned, the right relinquished and in love the brother's welfare considered of the foremost importance in the matter. Thus, the eighth chapter of I Corinthians closes (cf. v. 13).

In chapter 9, Paul illustrates how he applied this principle in a different context. In his missionary work (and, indeed, in his work at Corinth) he followed this principle. For the sake of unbelievers, young converts and the witness of the church, he laid aside his rights to marriage, to receiving pay under certain circumstances, etc., lest in any way he might hinder the progress of the gospel or become a stumbling block. (Note the recurring emphasis on rights in this chapter. Those who teach that we have no rights are wrong. God has granted rights of various sorts.)

There is, as I previously indicated, a resumption of the theme set forth in chapter 8. That begins in the middle of chapter 10. Paul reiterates his earlier points, and then discusses the role of conscience more fully. Let us consider what he says.

First, there is a summary: "Everything is lawful, but not all things are advantageous; all sorts of things are lawful, but not all things build up"

(10:23). Moreover, no Christian is to put himself or his interests first, but rather he is to have his brother's interests higher on his list (v. 24).

Then Paul considers various cases and applies his principles to each. These case studies are important because they show us how to use biblical principles in concrete situations:

1. Food sacrificed to idols may be eaten for one's own personal use if there is no danger of leading anyone astray in any manner (v. 25). Those who have no conscience against eating know that all such things belong to the Lord—not to idols or false gods (v. 26). So, when Paul says that he'll "never eat meat" (8:13), he means *in situations where it might cause another to sin.* It is clear that neither he nor others would refrain from personal use where there was no such danger.

2. If an unbeliever invites a Christian to dinner, the Christian is to eat whatever meat that is set before him and ask no questions. He is to raise no issue about whether this meat was offered to idols (v. 27). Why should he? He has no conscience about the matter.

3. However, in the third case, if someone (the Greek is *tis*=anybody—believer or unbeliever) else makes an issue of the matter saying, "This was offered in sacrifice" (or words to that effect), then the Christian should refuse it (v. 28). He does so for the sake of *others,* however, and not for his own sake (he has no conscience about eating *per se*). The other may regard the idol as a god or as contaminating the meat (cf. v. 28).

But this leads Paul to ask, "Why should my freedom be determined by another's conscience?" (v. 29). If I share a meal thankfully, why should I be criticized for eating that for which I gave thanks (vv. 29, 30)? Is Paul now contradicting what he said before? Is he now claiming rights that he said he would abandon under such circumstances? No, in these words he is taking the side of the reader who may object to what he has been teaching in chapter 8 and which he has just reaffirmed.

In verses 31ff. he answers those objections, and, in doing so, pushes the matter at least one step further along. He argues, you must "do everything for God's glory" (31b). When all is said and done, it isn't the brother's conscience, or even his welfare that is uppermost in the exercise of limits on your liberty. You must allow another's conscience to dictate *in order to glorify God.* If you become a stumbling block for *anyone*—Jew, Greek, believer—you thereby hurt His cause and dishonor God. As I (Paul) always adapt to the culture and situation in missionary work, even when it means that to do so puts me at a disadvantage personally, so too should you be willing to do so in whatever you do in order to please God. In this "imitate" me as you have seen me imitate Christ (11:1), who likewise put others first (cf. Phil. 2).

* * *

Let us now summarize what we have learned.
1. Situations arise in which the very same act may be sin for one person and not for another. This is not due to any relativism in biblical ethics, but to a relativism in the sinners who must follow them! The difference lies in knowledge, interpretations and attitudes. The best summary statement of the principle is found in Romans 14:23.
2. A Christian's personal freedom is limited by a consideration of whether or not the exercise of his freedom tempts a brother to stumble (sin) or gives an unbeliever cause to reject or criticize the gospel. In such cases an act thus becomes sin for him to do what under other circumstances would not be sin, not because of the act itself, but because of its adverse effects on others and on God's name.

* * *

These Pauline principles, as I stated earlier, are of great significance to Christian counselors. Often counselees will demand a yes/no answer to questions involving certain indifferent practices. Counselors must be careful not to give an unqualified "go ahead" signal before examining all the surrounding facts in the case, and (in particular) the knowledge and attitudes that form the standard in the counselee's conscience. Always try to determine where his conscience stands with reference to matters of this sort. A too quick response by the counselor could send the counselee out to sin.

On the other hand, counselors must maintain the right of a believer to do whatever the Bible permits *even when another believer doesn't like him to do so*. So long as his participation in a practice leads to no danger of others

12

following his example and thereby falling into sin, he may exercise his rights.[4]

Thus it is fair to say, as a final word, that Christians have liberty, but with a limit.

A Note on Questionable Sexual Practices

Regularly, in counseling, in question and answer periods and in private conversations, I am asked about various sexual practices. The questioner usually asks: "Is such-and-such a practice legitimate? I don't know because the Bible doesn't mention it."

Has God left us without guidance on these matters? In making decisions, is one purely on his own?

No. There are both a broad principle and a narrower one that pertain to the question; we are not without guidance.

A. The broad principle: Here is what I have called the "holding principle" (see also *More than Redemption* [Phillipsburg, N.J.: Presbyterian and Reformed, 1979]). According to Romans 14:23, whatever is not of faith is sin. It is *not* right to participate in any practice if one either

(1) thinks it is sin to do so, or,

(2) thinks it might be sin to do so (doubts).

Either way he sins, not because a given practice necessarily is wrong (it may be legitimate in God's sight) but because the person *thinks* it is or *might be wrong and does it anyway*. That *attitude* toward God is itself sinful.

B. The narrow principle: In I Corinthians 7:4, Paul says, "The wife doesn't have authority over her own body; rather it is her husband who does. Also, the husband doesn't have authority over his own body; rather it is the wife who does." This basic principle of love—that in sexual relations one's task is to please his marriage partner, not himself, has a number of ramifications. First, it eliminates autoeroticism, including masturbation. Secondly, it allows the other person's needs to dictate the frequency of sexual relations,

---

4. So often the passages in I Cor. and Rom. have been misused to justify curtailing another's freedom simply because another—who will tell you he is not tempted to follow the example— merely objects to a practice. The two things—offending/causing to offend—must be distinguished. Objection to and influence over are two quite distinct concepts.

and, thirdly, it means *one may never demand of his/her partner any practice that he/she finds questionable or abhorrent.* So God *has* spoken on the subject. If the *principle of love*—putting others first—is combined with the *holding principle,* there can never be a time when the partners get into arguments or impasses over such practices. It simply won't happen. It will be, rather, like two cars arriving simultaneously at a four-way stop sign and each driver saying "You first." Each partner will respect the wishes and the conscience of the other.

So, the Christian counselor will not speculate about the numerous practices that people ask about. Rather, he will articulate these general principles. How much better to have guiding principles like these that

(1) stress *love toward a partner* in solving problems;

(2) stress one's *attitude toward God* in doing so, rather than merely receiving a list of dos and don'ts.

In such situations, God wants us not only to obey and do the right thing, but to grow closer to Him and to one another in coming to decisions.

3

Counseling the Disabled

"How do you help a disabled person? Isn't it harder for him to make it in life? Isn't it cruel to talk to him about responsibility, the way you nouthetic counselors always seem to do?"

Those questions are good ones. And there may be some disabled persons reading this who need to hear the answers to them. Those who live with disabled persons surely do, and those who minister to them in some way or counsel them also should be interested in a biblical approach to the disabled.

Let's begin by admitting that the disabled person's lot is hard. Counselors must never minimize the tragedies of life and the effects of the curse on human life. And, we may also acknowledge that the more debilitating and the more highly visible the disability, the harder life becomes. These are givens; there is no way around them. All that I say must take these givens into consideration.

But we also must recognize that sympathizing and making allowances alone will not solve the disabled person's problems. Indeed, sometimes these very approaches make things harder still. Sympathy, if not coupled with true help, and making allowances that have nothing to do with the disability itself, can be downright destructive, no matter how well meant.

Precisely because disabilities usually make life harder, the truly empathetic counselor will *stress* biblical responsibility and *not* allow the disabled counselees to "get away with" anything. It is all too easy for them to adopt sinful patterns by which they wring sympathy from others *in order to be allowed to escape responsibilities* that they could and should assume. The counselor will be on the alert for manipulative patterns and, for their own benefit, will confront disabled persons concerning them. How does he do so?

One way is to point out that Paul was a disabled person; yet he never shirked his responsibilities. His "thorn in the flesh," he said, "slapped him around" (II Cor. 12:7). Many disabled persons can identify with that sort of

15

language. But despite this serious affliction, Paul continued to assume every obligation that he physically could; and throughout he maintained a proper attitude toward his disability. How did he do so?

1. He prayed about it; three times he asked God to remove it. But He didn't (v. 8; the word used means "pleaded"). Disabled persons can identify with that too. Then he stopped. Why?

2. Because he began to interpret his disability. It was given to keep him from becoming "conceited" over the great revelations he had received (v. 7). Counselors must help counselees to interpret their disabilities in a positive manner too as God-given and for a significant purpose. Such interpretations may be tentative or partial, but ought to be forthcoming.

3. Through the disability he found special help from Christ, who is willing to manifest (or make "fully evident") His power through our weakness. Here, in itself, is a significant purpose and a tremendous ministry opened wide for every disabled person (cf. v. 9). Paul was so happy for everyone to see Christ's power evident that he could even become happy about his affliction and "boast" about his "weakness" (v. 9b).

4. This led to contentment (v. 10). There was no continued agonizing "Why? Why this? Why me? Why now?," etc. No, the matter was resolved. God sent it to manifest Christ's power in Paul's life, and he was satisfied for it to do so. That was his conclusion of the matter. So too, the biblical counselor must lead the disabled counselee into just such a ministry of manifest power, and into such a state of contentment as goes along with it.[1]

"But," someone objects (I can almost hear it as I write), "Paul wasn't an invalid. Is it proper to say that he was a disabled person?"

We can be disabled in many ways. Paul's difficulty was quite serious. He had some sort of eye difficulty. That we know. (Perhaps he was partially blind.) In Galatians he says, "You know that it was because of physical sickness that I announced the good news to you. . . (4:13). N.B., the illness didn't keep Paul from fulfilling his God-given responsibility. He continues: ". . . my physical condition was a trial to you," but, he notes, ". . . if it had been possible you would have gouged out your eyes and given them to me" (vv. 14, 15). And, at the conclusion of the letter he points out, "Notice the large letters in which I am writing to you with my

---

1. The story of Joni Eareckson is a modern account of just such a ministry.

16

own hand" (6:11). Probably these words refer to the last paragraph or two since Paul tells us elsewhere, "I [Paul] write this greeting with my own hand, and this is the indication in every letter that I have written it" (II Thess. 3:17).

We must conclude that Paul had continuing serious eye trouble that was so debilitating that he could not pen an entire letter (unless Galatians is an exception over which he must have agonized) but had to use an amanuensis. That kind of a problem is a disability. I say it again, Paul was a disabled person from whom other disabled persons can learn much.

The very fact that we know so little about his disability, and must piece it together in the way that we do, is the surest indication that Paul did not use it in a manipulative way.

What else must the counselor help the handicapped, or disabled, person to do? In addition to the basic considerations already mentioned, I want to point out that the essential nature of a disability is that it *limits* the one disabled. Counselors should discuss thoroughly this matter of limitation with counselees since it is of such central import. Handicaps, as in Paul's case, always limit (Paul could not write whole letters himself, often must have been hindered in travel, etc.). But consider this:

1. Everyone has limitations. Some are less visible than others. One person has limited intelligence, another has a lack of coordination that keeps him from excelling in sports. Others cannot walk; some have no ability to carry a tune. A disabled person is disabled more than others *only in degree*. He is by no means to be considered *a special sort of person*. Like anyone else, he is first and above all else, a human being, created in the image of the living God. The designation "disabled" fits him in some special sense—rather than all of us—only because of the extent to which his disability limits him, its high visibility (i.e., in some way it calls attention to itself), etc. What is extraordinary about a disabled person, then, is in degree, not in kind; it is, finally, a matter of the extent or degree of the limitation involved that marks him out. Counselors who think of their own limitations, and how Christ has enabled them to handle them, already know the *basic* approach to use with the handicapped (II Cor. 1:4).[2]

---

2. N.B., Paul does not say that we can counsel only those who have the same affliction, but those with *any* affliction. The principles and the power are the same.

2. This basic approach to limitation as something common to all is important because the disabled person (labeled as such on signs in parking lots, in rest rooms, etc.) is in danger of growing resentful over his (as he may come to see it) unique problem. (It isn't; see my booklet on I Cor. 10:13, *Christ and Your Problems* [Phillipsburg, N.J.: Presbyterian and Reformed, 1971].) Counselors must strongly affirm his commonalities over his differences. The temptation to become bitter, the temptation to indulge in self-pity, the temptation to manipulate and the temptation to rationalize one's failure to assume his proper responsibilities may all be traced to a common root: a focus by the disabled counselee on his uniqueness and on his disabilities, rather than on his commonalities and his abilities.[3]

3. Counselors, therefore, must help him assess the God-given abilities that he *does* have, the possibilities for productive work and ministry that do exist, etc. Limitations must be viewed not as disabling the person *in toto*. (He is *not* a disabled *person*, but rather, a *person* who is disabled in only *some* respects.) Limitations are necessary for success. The scientist who achieves something significant limits himself to a narrow field of study. He purposely neglects much that he could be doing in order to focus and concentrate his interests, studies and endeavors. This is true of all highly successful persons who contribute something to the world.

But many of us, with greater abilities, achieve very little because we never learn the lessons of *self*-limitation. The person with disabilities has no such problem; God has limited him already, thus *enabling* him more easily to focus and concentrate on those areas in which his abilities lie. If he only will see it and enter into it, the person with a handicap can capitalize on this limitation. For him the problem is simplified: he doesn't need to decide about what he must eliminate; providentially, much has been eliminated for him already.

Persons who recognize these facts and, in imitation of Paul, handle their limitations righteously, do not fall into the many pits that line the pathway of the disabled. There is, for example, the self-centered attitude that says, "Now look out for me; I have a disability, you know. Put me first in line." Of course, as he thinks this way and tells everybody else such things, he is

---

3. Anyone, even those with far less visible disabilities who would never be labeled "disabled" or "handicapped," may focus on his limitations and become resentful. Many do; counselors meet them daily.

also telling himself. Pretty soon he believes it. Then, when people don't go to extraordinary lengths to accommodate him, he gets angry or sulks. Such talk is evidence of a problem, and should be noted (at length—at the appropriate time) by the counselor.

There is always someone with a greater (or, at least, very different) disability than your counselee. Tell him about that person. Tell him, "Here is someone for whom you might *care,* whom you may be able to help, to whom you may be able to minister." Moreover, many of us who are not so visibly disabled as to be labeled (a heinous practice) need his help. The counselor's task will be to enlighten him about his potential for ministry and to help him gear it into practical activity. Every "disabled" person, like every other Christian, should minister to someone else. But, it is especially good when he can minister to those who do not bear the label, but who are thought of as "normal." Self-centeredness is sin, even for a disabled person. For many, it is the most disabling factor of all.

Self-pity often leads to complacency, depression, worry, and sickness. Self-pitying persons let responsibilities slide, then blame the fact on their disabilities (or the failure of others). When a disabled Christian becomes depressed through self-pity, bitterness and the like as a result of following his feelings rather than assuming his responsibilities (no matter how he feels), his problem is no different from that of any other Christian; and he must be brought to see that. His disabilities never excuse him from the responsibilities that truly fit his abilities.

What does a disabled Christian need? He needs to be challenged to live up to his full capacity in the service of Christ, to the glory of God—exactly as every other Christian does. Even if he is totally paralyzed, he has *time,* the greatest natural gift of God. He must use that time profitably, perhaps in prayer. Perhaps he can record messages to missionaries, pastors or others on tape, etc. He must discover (and counselors must help him to do so) profitable uses for his time. (It is wrong to devote most of one's waking moments to watching TV.)[4]

Remember Paul's point: the disabled person is in some sense "weak" (Paul's word for what we call "disabled"). That weakness is the most fertile soil of all in which the fruit of God's power may grow.

---

4. Though it is possible that he could become a TV critic for a Christian publication.

4

Is Transactional Analysis OK?

Frequently I have been asked to comment on the movement known as Transactional Analysis (T.A., for short). This request often is occasioned by concern over the inroads that this pagan counseling system is making among Christian churches. On that point alone let me say a word before I go on.

It is tragic to see how some Christians grasp frantically for every clever new approach that comes down the pike. Among other things, this shows the theological weakness of those who do so. They seem not to be able to discover and evaluate the presuppositions, principles and practices of a system in order to determine whether it is essentially biblical or anti-biblical. (Some, of course, may not have any concern to do so if their own presuppositions are of an eclectic bent.) Usually this inability stems from the deplorable fact that pastors have been trained in seminaries (too often the fountainheads of all sorts of problems in our churches) to think, do exegesis and theology *abstractly*. They do not know how to use the fruits of their studies in the Bible to discuss, dissect and decide upon the everyday problems of life. They have been trained to handle "theological issues," never realizing that theology is for living (cf. Titus 1:1b).[1] They do not know how to translate doctrine and exegesis into counseling, so they eagerly search for some system that will enable them, they think (wrongly) to help counselees. Most of the seminaries that turn out such men have, themselves, adopted the eclectic spirit in counseling.

Whatever else may be behind the eclectic spirit, we see much evidence of its existence today among Bible-believing people in churches and (particularly) in educational institutions. The widespread acceptance of T.A. (or elements of it) is a case in point.

---

1. For much more on how doctrine may be related to life, see my book *More than Redemption* (Phillipsburg, N.J.: Presbyterian and Reformed, 1979), which is a textbook on the theology of counseling.

Since from its inception T.A. has, in its principles and in their formulations, exhibited a hostility toward the Christian faith, and since T.A. constitutes an attack upon all the fundamental principles of authority, one might conclude that T.A. would be rejected out of hand by conservative Christians. Such is not the case. How come? Because, as I noted, Christians fail to see the presuppositional stance of a movement and its effects because they do not know how to discover these through an analysis of the operative principles embedded in the practices of the system.

Here, there is no opportunity to fully expose and evaluate the system. Therefore, I shall focus on two facts and let the reader judge for himself whether or not the system merits the acceptance of the Christian church. It is not necessary to know whether a piece of fruit is rotten (and if so, where) or whether it tastes sour or sweet, etc., if one has discovered that it is poisonous. That fact alone provides more than adequate reason for rejecting it. We shall look at the poison in the T.A. apple.[2]

Now for the two poisonous facts.

1. What the Bible says can be done only by the Spirit of God working by His Word, T.A. asserts it can do without either. It is, therefore, in conflict and in competition with Christianity.

2. What the Bible says man needs as an authority structure for living, T.A. attacks and attempts to destroy. T.A., thereby, is in rebellion against God's sovereign authoritative structures in the world.

If these two positions can be shown to be true of T.A., then it should be plain that Christians must reject and repel goals, principles and methods of T.A. as a pagan substitute for the Christian faith.

But first, let us take a glimpse at the background of T.A.

Eric Berne, the founder of the movement, was a close friend of Erik Erikson, the neo-Freudian who wrote the shockingly inaccurate and prejudicial study of Martin Luther. Berne was strongly influenced by Erikson. Erikson, in contrast to Freud, emphasized the primacy of the *ego* over the *id*. Yet he remained generally within the Freudian camp. Berne, in this, reflects Erikson. But Berne had a clever mind and a way with words that is

---

2. For those wishing to do so, T.A. can be investigated most thoroughly in the writings of Eric Berne, Claude Steiner and Tom (I'm OK, You're OK) Harris.

unparalleled in the field of counseling. He took some of the basic concepts of neo-Freudianism, mixed them with some of his own ideas (and the ideas of others) and repackaged them in new, very attractive wrappers. To this old product he gave a new name, Transactional Analysis.

Berne no longer spoke in crusty, formidable terms about the *id*, the *ego* and the *superego*. Rather, he renamed them Parent (superego), Adult (ego) and Child (id). This transformation of the Freudian product made it much more salable. The new image modernized Freud; Berne began to talk about "games people play," "life scripts," and used catchy titles ("Ain't It Awful") for these games and scripts. The face-lift gave remarkable new life to limping old theories.

Following Berne's lead, Steiner and (especially) Harris have continued to popularize the viewpoint under similar attractive themes: *Scripts People Live* (Steiner); *I'm O.K.—You're O.K.* (Harris). Harris is the greatest popularizer of the three. It was he who spread the movement widely among the general public. Steiner still retains much of the stiffer, more academic approach from which Berne, in spite of his racy vocabulary, never quite separated.

Now, let us turn to the two areas that I have isolated. In our archeological dig we shall send down but a couple of shafts from which we shall gather samples.

First, I said that T.A. is competitive to Christianity because it claims to provide what the Bible says only Christianity can achieve. And it sees no need for the truth of the Word or the power of the Spirit.

Consider Harris' words,

> I believe that Transactional Analysis may provide an answer to the predicament of man.[3]

Something of the messianic claims and spirit of T.A. can be seen in this statement, which (in its context) clearly indicates the fact. *Time* Magazine wrote this about Harris' book:

> The book itself goes so far as to suggest that it may be able to save man and civilization from extinction.[4]

---

3. Harris, *I'm OK—You're OK*, p. 258.
4. *Time*, Aug. 10, 1973, p. 45.

The writer of the *Time* article observes that

> . . . Harris is convinced that only those who believe the "truth" of transactional analysis can win the battle against neurosis,

and quotes him as saying,

> You have to have absolute faith that T.A. is true; otherwise you'll lose.[5]

These calls for truth and absolute faith are, it seems, religious demands no less exacting than that of Him who said "I am the . . . truth . . . no man comes to the Father but by Me."

And, coupled with that is the idea that this salvation of mankind (and individuals) is realized in those who agree "that the not-OK posture is an illusion."[6] Theologically speaking, that means that man's sinful nature is denied. As Steiner continually puts it, you must *"Trust human nature and believe in your children."*[7] Indeed, the thrust of the movement is that success comes when you deny the reality of non-OKness (sin). Like traditional Freudianism, T.A. thinks that guilt feelings can be removed by denying sin. T.A. approaches human problems humanistically, rejecting the need for grace and a Savior. To accept T.A. principles is, therefore, to deny Jesus Christ and His cross any place. As a matter of fact, this conflict goes even deeper. God, whom Berne calls Santa Claus, is called an illusion. The would-be T.A. counselor is warned that "it takes enormous power to shatter these primal illusions," and is told that

> In order for the patient to get better, his illusion, upon which his whole life is based, must be undermined so that he can live in a world which is here today . . . the script analyst . . . [must] tell his patients finally that there is no Santa Claus.[8]

Clearly these samples show how T.A. is at odds with Christianity and is in the business of trying to undermine faith in God while seeking to establish belief in man—and (even more specifically) unquestioned trust in its own dogmas.

---

5. Ibid.
6. Alan Reuter, "Psychology and Theory: A Return to Dialog," *Concordia Theological Monthly* 44, no. 3 (May, 1973).
7. Claude Steiner, *Scripts People Live* (New York: Grove Press, 1974), p. 309.
8. Eric Berne, *What Do You Say After You Say Hello?* (New York: Bantam Press, 1973), pp. 152, 153.

"But why don't you think that God can reveal truth even through men and systems like this one in His common grace? Isn't all truth God's truth?" One grows weary of such questions; but questioners seem never to grow weary of asking them. By the theological gymnastics that are used to justify T.A. (and other counseling systems that, in fact, are in direct competition and conflict with Christianity), the door of common grace is opened widely enough to admit even avowed atheism as in some respects "a good and useful system" that we "ought not reject out of hand," from which we may "learn a good bit" and from which we most certainly may adopt "any number of helpful methods."

Well, of course God works in common grace! Certainly all truth is God's truth. But what has that to do with T.A.? Such arguments are specious; they beg the question. The issue is this:

1. Is T.A., as it claims, truth (we may not simply *assume* so as eclectic persons who misuse the words "common grace" so often do)? We must ask, does T.A. reveal truth from God or is it a godless system set up to rival Christianity?[9] That question cannot be answered by *asserting* it; saying something is true doesn't make it so. There is a way, however, to determine whether T.A. is a medium by which God reveals truth and that is to ask, Does T.A. square with the Bible? God never contradicts in common grace what He teaches in special grace (i.e., in the Scriptures).

2. We can be sure that God did not set up a system in common grace to do what He says (in the Bible) can be done only by the Spirit working through the ministry of the Word. Common grace never *replaces* special grace. God is not a God of confusion, telling us one thing in the Scriptures and something different somewhere else.

All of us find much help in those truths that do come through God's common grace. However, the area with which we are dealing is not one in which we should expect the same sort of help that we receive in other areas of life. Human living is the area to which the *Bible* addresses itself. In the Scriptures, and in the Scriptures alone, can one discover how to love God and one's neighbor (and that is the core of what counseling is all about). And

---

9. I have shown how pagan counseling systems fail to measure up to the claim of common grace and, indeed, constitute systems that propagate the "counsel of the ungodly" in my book, *More than Redemption*.

24

these very Scriptures teach that such love begins and ends with Jesus Christ. Yet T.A. says,

Dogma is the enemy of truth and the enemy of persons,[10]

and

Truth is not something which has been bound in a black book.[11]

Can we believe that this sort of thing is a blessing of God's common grace, or that it could be the channel for it? Can a system based on such views be integrated with Christianity, as some think?

Certainly not! They are wrong; God told us that all things necessary for life and godliness have been given in special revelation. Surely, generations of Christians prior to Berne and Harris were not wrong in believing so! Any addition to the Scriptures claiming to better tell us how to live (not to speak of substitutions and conflicting views) therefore must be suspect. Did Jesus Christ have all He needed to live a perfect life and to become the perfect Counselor from the O.T. Bible alone? Or, was He lacking in much that T.A. could have taught Him?

We have been seeing how my second charge against T.A. holds up: T.A. attacks the authority structure God gave us by viewing truth as relative. It will have no absolutes. Children must not be restricted, but left free to do as they please.[12] The authority of God in the home is eroded as it is in the church. The authority of God Himself is opposed. Authority demands a submissive relationship, the kind that is undercut by T.A.'s goal of autonomy. The T.A. concept of the naughty parent, whose authority must be rejected by the Adult shows this clearly.

Consider the following:

Truth is a growing body of data of what we observe to be true.[13]

This bald statement taken in conjunction with Harris' rejection of truth in a "black book" leads to a subjectivism in which T.A. is found to be superior

---

10. Harris, op. cit., p. 260. Of course, T.A. dogma is excepted.

11. Ibid., p. 265. It is perfectly clear what book the writer had in mind.

12. Cf. Steiner, op. cit., pp. 303-9. He says that children must "not be prevented from doing things they want to do" (p. 306).

13. Harris, op. cit., p. 265.

to the Bible! On this basis, of course, there is no final standard or authority beyond one's self. Indeed, we do not have to guess at any such conclusion; we are told so frankly and openly:

> . . . when morality is encased in the structure of relit is essentially Parent. It is dated, frequently unexamined, and often contradictory. . . . Parent morality . . . impedes the formulation of a universal ethic. The position I'm OK—You're OK is not possible if it hinges on your accepting what I believe.[14]

In speaking of what he considers to be the true religious experience, Harris wrote,

> I believe that what is emptied is the Parent.[15]

From this brief survey (much more could be said) it should be evident to all concerned Christians that T.A. is incompatible with the Christian faith and that those who become involved in its tenets do so at great peril.

---

14. Ibid., pp. 260, 261.
15. Ibid., p. 268. Remember, the parent is religion, authority, dogma, etc.

5

How to Win an Unsaved Wife to Christ

A listener to my radio broadcast once wrote:

> Have been enjoying your short messages. Lately you've been talking about the way that wives can win their unsaved husbands for Christ. Many authors and speakers deal with the above topic. I haven't heard any tackle the opposite—how a saved husband can win his wife to Christ. Do we just reverse what we hear about wives' roles? It is just "love your wives, as Christ loved His Church"?

The question is a good one. The listener is right; we do hear little or nothing about this matter. One reason for that is that the Scriptures speak so much more fully about what wives must do.[1] But, as we shall see, the question is a matter of emphasis, not a question of exclusion.

We all know that in I Peter 3:1-6, a passage that I was discussing on the radio when this letter was written, Peter clearly outlines how a Christian wife is to behave in order to please God and (possibly) win her unsaved husband to the Lord. There he stresses the need for aggressive submission, a beautiful inner spirit and respectful obedience in doing good.

At first it seems that there is no comparable instruction for Christian husbands. Perhaps, in Peter's day (as in ours) there were more wives than husbands in this position. But, as I said, Peter is concerned mainly about the issue of submission to an unsaved authority under whom one might suffer for her faith. But what passages tell the Christian husband what to do?

Paul mentions the problem in I Corinthians 7:12ff.: Apart from expressing his concern for winning an unsaved wife to Christ, and requiring husbands to

---

1. In I Peter 3 the *emphasis* is on the wife of an unsaved husband because, in the context, Peter is dealing principally with various authority situations in which the believer suffers in submission.

continue living with them in order to win them, he says nothing more about *how* to do so. When he speaks of the unsaved wife as being "sanctified" by her Christian husband, he does not mean that the wife is automatically saved because of her association with him or anything else of the sort. The word *sanctified* has a wide band of uses in the Scriptures. Fundamentally it means to "set apart," and can be used even of the pots and pans that were used in the OT temple. These were *special* (*set apart* from others) and could be used nowhere else and for no other purposes than those for which they had been set apart. So, too, the unsaved wife who lives with a Christian husband is in a *special* or *privileged* position. She lives in constant contact with one in whom the Spirit is at work, with one who is praying for her salvation and with one who not only can instruct her in the gospel, but who (in his daily living) can demonstrate what Jesus Christ has done for him. Truly, she is in a sanctified (or special) situation in that covenant home on which God promises His special blessings. This teaching should be of great encouragement to a Christian husband who is married to an unbelieving wife.

But the question remains, *"How* does he go about demonstrating Christ to his wife?"* The listener is on the right track in making the suggestion that he did: "Do we just reverse what we hear about the wife's role? . . . Do we just love our wives as Christ loved the church?" However, two comments must be made:

1. Let's remove those "justs" from his suggestions. Winning a wife by one's life isn't a snap—as those words might indicate. It means proper attitudes, hard work, prayer, obedience to God and patient endurance and persistence. It will demand everything of him. And—of utmost importance—he can never do any of this as a gimmick to win his wife. He must do it *because God says so, to please Him*—whether his wife becomes a Christian or not.

2. There is more "how to" than at first might seem available to the casual reader of the Scriptures. And, perhaps surprisingly, it is in I Peter 3:7, immediately following the directions given to Christian wives.

Looking at I Peter 3:7, we must notice first the word "likewise." Clearly, this word (like its counterpart in v. 1) points back to the behavior of Jesus Christ described at the end of chapter 2. (See my commentary on I Peter, *Trust and Obey* [Phillipsburg, N.J.: Presbyterian and Reformed, 1978], for more details.) But it also serves the function of linking the directions given to wives (vv. 1-6) with those given to husbands (v. 7). Both take their impetus from the same source. Both sets of directions tell Christians how to win lost spouses; both, therefore, point to living out respective roles properly.

What does I Peter 3:7 require? That husbands live with their wives

> in an understanding way, showing respect for the woman as you would for a fragile container, and as joint heirs of the grace of life, so that your prayers may not be interrupted.

Echoes of Paul's better known requirements for loving leadership, as the head of the home, assuming and fulfilling all of the responsibilities of that headship, willingness to die (if need be) for one's wife (as Christ died for the church) and a desire to treat her as one's self,[2] may all be found in Peter's lesser known words, plus some other elements. It is those other elements, which constitute the "how to," to which we now turn.

Paul's call for love—a love like Christ had for His church—is often held out, and rightly so. But little is said about *how* one may begin to love his wife as Christ loved the church. Frequently (but not often enough) the point is made that this love is *unconditional,* i.e., it does not depend on anything in the one who is loved (cf. Rom. 5:6, 8, 10). Its source, its impetus, etc., is wholly within the one who loves, who (like Christ) determines to *set* his love on his wife *regardless* of whether there is anything loving, lovely or lovable about her (the church, before becoming such, was weak, sinful, rebellious). But still, *how* does one love like that? Specifically, *how* does he show unconditional love? Where does he begin?

A step closer to the answer is the observation (made even less frequently) that love isn't (first of all) an emotion; in the first instance love is giving. One loves an unlovely person as Christ did—by *giving* Himself (Eph. 5:25). One loves a hungry or thirsty enemy by *giving* (something to eat; a cup of cold water). That is to say, one *gives* whatever it is that he has that the one on whom he sets his love needs. That is closer to an operational answer; but what of the husband who says, "I don't know *what* my wife wants. I don't know how to please her; I simply don't understand her at all"? How does he begin to love (i.e., begin to give)?

Here is where I Peter 3:7 becomes most practical. Peter insists that

---

2. Cf. Eph. 5:25-33. For a detailed study of the passage, see my book, *Christian Living in the Home* (Phillipsburg, N.J.: Presbyterian and Reformed, 1972).

husbands must "live with" their wives "in an understanding way." His focus is on the fact that love—intelligent giving of one's time, possessions or self—grows out of understanding.

"But," he may insist, "you'll never understand a woman." That old cliché has done much harm. Like many other false sayings by which people live, this one has helped to destroy many marriages. If God commands Christian husbands to understand their wives, then it is possible as well as necessary for them to do so. But until both the possibility and the necessity of doing it are accepted by a husband, we may be sure that he will fail in any (half-hearted, hope-against-hope) attempts that he may make. God never commands His children to do anything that He fails to provide directions and power (in His Word and by His Spirit) to accomplish. We must believe this and obediently avail ourselves of these provisions. Well, then, how does one understand a wife?

The answer lies in the Greek words that have been translated "in an understanding way." Literally, they read "live with your wives *according to knowledge.*" Many husbands have been living for years in nearly total ignorance of all the true concerns, felt needs, etc., that their wives have.

"OK, but how does one obtain this knowledge?"

How do you get knowledge about something else? You seek it, arrange ways of getting it, etc.; in short, you do research to obtain it.

"Research my wife?"

Why not? Most men have spent more time researching far less important matters.

"Well. . . ."

You could begin by interviewing her.

"Interview her? How do you interview a wife?"

First, you set an appointment.

"Ask my *wife* for an appointment?"

Certainly. You wouldn't think of barging in on a client at any old time to ask questions whether or not he was prepared, or whether or not he had the time, would you?

"Well, . . . I guess not . . . but. . . ."

No buts about it. Your wife deserves every bit as much consideration and more.

"But when I try to talk to her I get nowhere. . . ."

Perhaps one of the major reasons is that, like many couples, you do it at inappropriate times and in inappropriate ways. That's one reason for making a definite appointment that suits both of you for a time and place you set aside for this purpose only. Make sure there will be no interruptions. Then, you might begin to get somewhere.

"But she won't tell me what I want to know. I've tried before and. . . ."

You've never tried doing so on an appointment, have you?

"No, but. . . ."

Well, then you don't know whether she will or won't. Besides, I haven't finished making my full suggestion.

"Go ahead."

Well, making an appointment to interview your wife, rather than trying to find out what you want to know about her when you both are rushed and on the run, will create different conditions. Making the appointment itself ought to show her that you mean business.

"OK, so I make the appointment. What do I do when I interview her? I haven't the slightest idea where to begin or what to say. What next?"

The answer to that is *preparation*. You must spend the better part of every waking free moment for at least a week before you interview her, thinking about what you want to know about her concerns, joys, fears, expectations, likes, dislikes, and whatever else you want to know. And you should write down every question and work hard on how you word each one to make sure you do it well. (I'll be glad to go over the list with you beforehand to make suggestions on wording or content.) When your wife sees what extensive preparations you have made, she will be much more likely to understand that you are serious about this matter and give you good responses. And, incidentally, let me point out a very significant fact—you will have already begun to express love toward her by giving. You will have given of your time and thought to this list. I'd be sure to have *at least* 25 well-thought-through, well-worded, fairly specific questions on that list.

"Well, it just might work. At least, it is worth a try. Do you have any other ideas for understanding a woman?"

Yes. Another thing you can do is *observe* her.

"How do I go about doing that?"

Well, the next time the two of you go to the department store together. . . .

"I don't go to department stores with her!"

Then let me put it differently: The *first* time that you go to the department store with her, as you pass through (let us say) the china section and she stops to admire a plate, *observe*. If she lingers with it, holds it up to the light, looks at it from various angles, etc., make a note of it—she likes it. Then, if she stops, looks at it again on the way out, put a mental check mark next to your note and buy her a piece of it for your anniversary. You can also observe her needs, her concerns, etc.

"What else do you suggest?"

I'll give you one more idea; you can add others if you like: Use feedback. For one week, do one small thing for your wife daily—just to please her.

"Feedback? Sometimes I get too much of that from her!"

Well, what I have in mind will tend to generate useful feedback if you do it well. Be sure that you give plenty of thought each day to what you do for her. Try to determine in your mind, from past experience, what she might like and what she might not. Then do it. But make it something small, just in case you fail to hit the target! And, by the way, do something that doesn't cost any money. (It's too easy just to buy some flowers on the way home from work. It might be better to stop along the road and pick some dried wild flowers instead.) At any rate, whatever you do, *give*. (Remember that's how love begins—with giving; cf. John 3:16; Gal. 2:20); give of your thought, your time, your effort. That is to say, give of your*self!*

"I can see some value in that—it gives me a chance to start thinking about her and expressing love in concrete ways by giving, but where, exactly, does the feedback come in?"

From the response you get to what you did. Be satisfied with "A" for effort (love) even if she "fails" you on the item itself. In other words, you will begin (as you put it) in "concrete ways" to discover what she likes and doesn't like by the feedback. Ask for an honest response, and be as satisfied with a negative one as you would with a positive one. During the first few weeks of this you are *mainly* interested in gathering data from feedback to help you to live with your wife in an understanding way. If you get positive or negative feedback it doesn't matter. Both help you achieve your goal of gathering significant *data* about your wife's likes and dislikes in order to understand her better. But as the understanding comes, you'll hit the target more and more, and the increase in positive feedback will make you aware of the fact. All along, your wife should be drawn closer to you (and you to her), not just because you do score a hit or two, but mainly because she sees you making such an effort. And, the more time, thought and effort you invest in your wife, the more your concern for her will grow: "Where your treasure is, there your heart will be also."

There is a second element in this verse for counselors to emphasize to Christian husbands. They must treat their wives as "weaker vessels" (KJV). When reading this, one husband responded, "Weaker vessel? You should have seen her throw the TV set across the room at me!!" The translation in my *Christian Counselor's NT* clears up the problem:

> showing respect for the woman as you would for a fragile container.

The verse doesn't call the woman a weaker vessel, but tells you to treat her with the same respect that you would give a fragile vase. This is compatible to Paul's "nourish and cherish" her. Husbands truly are to be *gentle*men to their wives.

Some men treat their wives like old tin garbage cans; Christian husbands verbally, physically, and in every other way, must treat their wives like a fragile vase—Ming dynasty!

Finally, notice that a husband also must treat his wife as a joint heir to the grace of life. She too has participated in bringing birth to his children and has a crucial influence upon them. If he doesn't want his prayers for her salvation and the salvation of his children hindered (lit., "cut off"), the Christian will honor his wife as God has commanded. He will respect her for who she is, bearing an equal relationship to their children, and for the sort of influence (for good or for ill) that she brings to bear on those children.

So, in conclusion, let us encourage Christian husbands about this matter, so that they will enthusiastically assume the responsibilities of loving headship in their homes, that their wives and children alike may see the evidence of Christ living in them and may come to faith in response to their prayers.

6

The Use of I Corinthians 13 in Counseling

In any number of places in my books I have referred to I Corinthians 13 as an important passage for Christian counselors to know and use. And I have commented on various verses in that chapter on occasion.[1] Yet nowhere have I discussed the chapter as a whole. That I propose to do here. I do not (however) intend to become involved in detailed exegesis. There are too many good commentaries on I Corinthians for me to do that. Rather, my emphasis will be on meaning (without giving arguments for why I have reached certain conclusions about the text I shall simply go ahead with my interpretations) and on the application of those meanings to counseling. Throughout I shall use *The New Testament in Everyday English* (the text of *The Christian Counselor's New Testament*[2]).

First, it is important to notice that I Corinthians 13 does not stand alone. It links chapters 12 and 14, and is an essential part of Paul's argument that there is something better (12:31) than the exercise of the special gifts of the Holy Spirit: love. Moreover, the discussion is a part of a larger context. The Corinthian church had been involved in unloving acts of disunity, lawsuits, etc. Surely, Paul's words in this chapter, though immediately dealing with their unloving use of gifts, also were calculated to meet the total situation. As such, the passage is pivotal and takes on an unparalleled importance in the letter. No wonder it has become a favorite among Christians. Yet, so often (like other favorites—the Lord's prayer, Ps. 23, etc.), it is known more for the familiar cadence of words, the melody of their structure, and the

---

1. Cf. *Shepherding God's Flock* (Phillipsburg, N.J.: Presbyterian and Reformed, 1980), pp. 18, 99, 178; *Lectures on Counseling* (Grand Rapids: Baker Book House, 1978), pp. 36, 243, 119f.; *The Manual* (Phillipsburg, N.J.: Presbyterian and Reformed, 1973), pp. 39, 153, 414, 369.

2. Also printed and published separately in a revised form without the counseling notes by Baker Book House, Grand Rapids, 1979.

general impression it makes than for its exact meanings and their applications to specific life situations. I propose to break out of the former and into the latter in this essay; unless the counselor does so, he will (1) contribute to faulty use of the Scriptures, and (2) fail to help counselees through the passage. So, then, it is *absolutely* necessary for the Christian counselor to do more than assign the reading of the chapter to counselees.[3]

The form of Paul's poem (or hymn) of love is striking. Rather than give any sort of formal definition (the Bible is not big on giving definitions, so why should I be?), Paul *describes* love in both positive and negative terms. In doing so, he makes but little direct application of his words to the problems that occasioned the poem; there are, of course, transitional, introductory sentences (12:31) and the simple hortatory statement in 14:1: "pursue love." So, while I Corinthians 13 plainly is an essential part of the discussion of the misuse of spiritual gifts, the passage stands squarely on its own two feet as the richest repository of biblical data on love, no matter what the problem lacking love may be.

Indeed, it may well be that Paul wrote the bulk of the words in this chapter for another occasion, or even as a hymn on love that, because of its appropriateness, he inserted at this point. Be that as it may, there is good warrant for considering the timeless truths taught here by themselves, and for making use of them in entirely different contexts, since there is nothing about the love passage that requires us to link it inextricably and solely to the loving use of gifts. Its form, as I have noted, gives no such impression but, rather, argues for seeing a more universal character in the poem.

I shall so treat it in this essay.

I shall not spend time here comparing and contrasting *agape* love (the word used throughout this chapter) with other biblical and extra-biblical terms for love as others have done.[4] That procedure, though it has its place, seems largely to miss the point. The principal way to learn about love, as Paul used the word in the New Testament, is to study I Corinthians 13, though, of course, in doing so the use of other portions of the Bible will be

---

3. Perhaps he could assign the reading of chapter 13 along with a part of my essay on love in this book.

4. For the best of such discussions, see B. B. Warfield, "The Terminology of Love in the N.T., II," *The Princeton Theological Review* 16, no. 2 (April, 1918):153ff. Avoid the several neoorthodox discussions that tend to lead astray.

appropriate (and at times necessary) in clarifying and deepening our understanding of I Corinthians 13. Consequently, I shall focus our attention on what Paul has said to us in the remarkable words that follow:

1   If I speak the languages of men and angels, but don't have love, I am a noisy gong or clanging cymbal.
2   And if I have a gift of prophecy and know all sorts of secrets and have all kinds of knowledge, and if I have all the faith that is necessary to move mountains but I don't have love, I am nothing.
3   And if I give food to the needy and even give away all my possessions, and if I allow my body to be burned, but I don't have love, I have gained absolutely nothing.

4   Love is patient, love is kind; it is not jealous. Love doesn't boast, isn't proud,
5   doesn't act in an ugly way, isn't self-seeking, isn't easily irritated, doesn't keep records of wrongs,
6   isn't happy about injustice but happily stands on the side of truth.
7   It covers all things, believes all things, hopes all things, endures all things.

8   Love never fails. If there are prophecies, they will be set aside; if there are languages, they will cease; if there is knowledge, it will be set aside.
9   We know in part and we prophesy in part,
10   but when that which is complete comes, that which is partial will be set aside.
11   When I was a child I spoke like a child, I reasoned like a child; but now that I have become a man I have set aside childish ways.
12   Now we see dimly as if looking in a bronze mirror, then face to face; now I know partially, but then I shall know fully just as I am fully known.
13   And now these three things continue: faith, hope, love; and the greatest of these is love.

The passage as a whole may be divided into three sections:

I.   Empty Substitutes for Love (1-3)
II. Essential Factors in Love (4-8)
III. Everlasting Aspects of Love (8-13)

I shall spend little time with sections 1 (vv. 1-3) or 3 (vv. 8-13) since they are not so directly descriptive of love itself. Rather, I shall concentrate on verses 4-8, in which many (not all) of the essential characteristics of love appear.

I. *Empty Substitutes for Love* (vv. 1-3)

None of the acts that are listed in verses 1 to 3 are wrong in themselves (indeed, each one of them can be *good when done in love*. As a matter of fact, that is the very point: N.B., the threefold qualifying phrase, "but don't have love," is what negates the act—not the nature of the act *per se*). These acts are valueless to one's self, to others or to God's kingdom *when separated from love*. Not only the ability to speak in an unknown language (tongue) without studying it, but the instant ability to speak *all* the languages on earth and in the heavens is useless (to Paul it's just so much meaningless noise) unless the use of that ability is motivated by love and used in a loving way for loving purposes (v. 1). In addition, even the use of the more profitable gift of prophecy (here defined as the knowledge, or understanding, of all sorts of hidden truths and the possession of deep truths revealed by God coupled with a powerful and active faith) is empty without love (v. 2). Indeed, more than that, the *possessor* of these coveted things is *himself* said to be "nothing" (*outhen*). He is an empty person, outwardly displaying knowledge and power, but a hollow person inwardly. And, he may engage in the giving of food or property (abstractly, out of guilt, under pressure, etc.) or even follow ascetic, self-centered courses of action (out of stubbornness, for fame or in unbiblical causes), leading ultimately to martyrdom (for such causes). But it is all (every bit of it) *profitless;* as far as Paul is concerned, it is mere waste. All these acts without love are worthless to the one doing them (though, in His providence, God may use them for His purposes). How much of what we have done must be junked when we evaluate it by such a standard!

Christians, therefore, must be concerned to act out of love—for God and for their neighbors. Love alone lifts such acts to a plane of eternal significance. Otherwise, they have but temporary and questionable value and meaning.

II. *Essential Factors in Love* (vv. 4-7).

I have already noted that the factors discussed in verses 4 to 7 do not constitute the whole of love. But they clearly are illustrative of it; i.e., they show us the sorts of things love does and doesn't do. They describe love *adequately* if not exhaustively. It is to this description, then, that the counselor will turn again and again in counseling, to find direction from God. That is why he must be utterly familiar with it. Let us consider each element in the passage separately. One way to think (or speak to a counselee) concretely about these factors in love is to see how each portrays some quality that we see in the Lord Jesus Christ. What we have here is, of course, a clear portrait of Him. I mention this, though I shall not elaborate on it.

The first factor is this:

(1) *"Love is patient."*

The word translated *patient* here is *makrothumia*. It means "long-tempered" and is the exact opposite of our expression "short-fused." It has to do with the restraint of anger, wrath and temper. A person with *makrothumia* has learned how to put up with others. He has learned to restrain himself in all sorts of life-situations. Apply it to the list of items in verses 1 to 3: What good does it do to speak in foreign languages if one says what he says in bad temper? What kind of a martyr is a short-fused martyr, etc.? It is clear, therefore, how important love is in giving value to these acts.

Very many counselees need this quality of *makrothumia*. There is no sense discussing all of the circumstances in which *patience* is essential in human lives. It is, perhaps, *the* factor in stressful situations that makes it possible for one to take whatever other biblical courses that are required of him. For details on how to obtain it, see my discussion of this in *More than Redemption* (Phillipsburg, N.J.: Presbyterian and Reformed, 1979) under my treatment of the fruit of the Spirit.[5]

A mother (or Christian school teacher) who shows no evidence of such patience with her children, for instance, may claim that she loves them—and indeed, that because of this love she is upset with them—but, according to Paul, to the extent that she loses her temper in disciplining them, she does not love them. Lack of patience is evidence of lack of love; patience—the willingness to restrain one's self for the sake of another—is one of the factors in love. A lack of patience indicates defective love.

Love thinks of the other person first; lack of patience puts one's self first

---

5. *More than Redemption* (Phillipsburg, N.J.: Presbyterian and Reformed, 1979), pp. 225ff.

and says, "Look what you did [to me]." Throughout this section, love will be shown to be a giving of one's self (time, interests, etc.) to another while giving up one's own rights, privileges, concerns, etc.

Love, in none of the statements that follow, is set forth as something that one *possesses* in the abstract (in and of itself, for himself). Rather, it is *always* seen as an attitude of self-giving for the sake of another. Love is always related to God or neighbor; it never stands alone.

(2) *"Love is kind."*

Again, I have considered this word (*chrestotes*) more fully in *More than Redemption.*[6] Consequently, I shall not develop it here. Let me say this about kindness, however: The word describes a condition in the lover that is opposed to all that is cruel or severe. Certainly, that which is deliberately cruel is outlawed. But also those severities that flow from thoughtlessness toward others (usually because of selfish concerns and pursuits) are eliminated as well. The *kind* person has a sort of gentleness that is active, not merely passive; it encompasses a desire to be outgoing and shows a vital interest in others and in their affairs. A *kind* person is one who cares about others enough so seek their welfare actively in some concrete way. Many counselees typically manifest self-centered traits, many of which involve severity and border on cruelty. Any call to love—the *one* call that all Christian counselors issue to every counselee in one way or another—therefore, *must* consider this matter. It may never be bypassed. No one claiming to love another can be either calculatingly (or thoughtlessly) harsh or cruel toward him.[7]

(3) *"Love is not jealous."*

This phrase is the beginning of a list of eight negative factors that Paul contrasts with love; each implies its opposite. When one loves another, he has no feelings of jealousy. He isn't sorry but, rather, joyous to see the other

---

6. Ibid.
7. Firmness is not necessarily cruelty or thoughtless severity. A loving firmness moved Paul to write I Corinthians, in which he shows firmness again and again. But that firmness grew out of deep concern for God and the Corinthian church.

possessing whatever good he has (again, the focus is on the welfare of the other rather than of one's self). There is no desire to lessen (in any way) the virtues, achievements or happiness of another. A lover *prefers* to put another before himself. Few counselees who learn to adopt this attitude toward others will have any serious difficulties left to counsel about. They may need direction, etc., but once given that, they will move ahead quickly to the solution of most of their interpersonal problems.

A jealous person is zealous (the two words are related) to hold onto and maintain his own rights and possessions at all costs. That is a sign or clear indicator of the presence of this unloving factor that chokes out the tender sprouts of love that from time to time spring forth. Let every counselor look for it and point it out in the lives of counselees whenever he encounters it.

On the other hand, a loving person wants to share what he possesses or has attained and enjoys helping others to attain whatever skills, status, etc., he himself has. Such a positive attitude *itself* would go far toward splitting apart many of the logjams that occur in counseling sessions. Whenever these standstills are experienced in counseling, check on this negative factor. As in all eight items, the way out begins with confession and repentance.[8] Following the softening of the heart through these, a counselor may assign the counselee specific ways in which (in his particular situation) he may begin to practice the positive actions implied as the opposites of this negative factor. Prayerful practice in time will lead to the enjoyment of seeing others possess and enjoy even that which he himself has never been able to attain.

(4) *"Love doesn't boast."*

The word has to do with *bragging, parading one's self before others.* Love doesn't seek such approval from others. The Adlerian emphasis on one's personal "need" for *significance* in the eyes of others has been imported into Christian circles by Larry Crabb and others. But Paul was not in agreement with Adler. Indeed, his views loudly clash with Adler's emphasis. A Christian doesn't need to feel significant in the eyes of others; he doesn't need fame (no matter how narrow its impact), admiration or applause. Rather, he will give proper praise to others; to be capable of doing that is his real "need."

---

8. Cf. the index in *More than Redemption* for discussions of confession and repentance.

Love doesn't show off. It makes no odious comparisons; it doesn't down others in order to lift self. Rather, it keeps quiet about even genuine achievements, preferring others to praise (if they will), but not *needing* their praise at all. Even when well-deserved praise comes, glory and honor is deflected from one's self in an *honest,* non-hypocritical effort to praise God, who made success possible.[9] This factor leads easily to the next.

(5) *"Love isn't proud."*

In love there is a humility (not a false humility, which is really a kind of pride) that always acknowledges behind achievement, beauty, brains, etc., the providential work of God. The humble man may acknowledge his successes, but he doesn't grow conceited because he knows that all that is worthwhile in his life has come from God through Jesus Christ. Such persons, again, don't demand much (rights, acknowledgment, praise, significance). Instead, their stock in trade is thankfulness. The counselor who wants to help a counselee to overcome the problem of boastfulness will focus on teaching him to acknowledge God's hand in all things and to thank Him for them.

(6) *"Love doesn't act in an ugly way."*

Coming to verse 6 we encounter a word that is related to *shame.* The unloving person will do things, say things, assume attitudes of which he (or others) will later be ashamed. Love never acts in an ugly, shameful way— with violence, foul language or anything else disgraceful. Love is concerned, therefore, about *manner* as well as matter. Love never offends by indelicate or crude acts and words. Certainly the use of four-letter "shock" words that some counselors seem to stock and use in good supply is to be condemned (as well as in the way counselees must learn to deal with one another) as unloving. How counselors who indulge in such practices expect to help counselees become more loving by their poor example is beyond me. Love, in contrast, works hard at doing always what is fitting, appropriate and mannerly (many parts of our land have lost all sense of that which is

---

9. That is not to say that one may not accept such appreciation with thanks. But (at the very least, in his heart) one may not focus on himself primarily or to the exclusion of God.

appropriate and mannerly), so long as these ways do not conflict with God's standards. Love tries always to do that which the Bible calls *fine*.[10]

(7) *"Love isn't self-seeking"* (cf. 10:24, 33).

Whatever love does, it accomplishes in a disinterested way. That is to say, it seeks the other person's welfare and does not calculate what benefits (or lack of benefits) may accrue to one's self in return. There is no boomerang thinking. Counselors continually must make it clear that counselees may not do what they do for others as a gimmick to gain certain personal ends. Perhaps no other sinful tendency intrudes itself more frequently into faulty Christian living. One sees it all the time in counseling sessions. Counselees, in one way or another, will say, "If I do this, what's in it for me?" Again and again they must be challenged to do what God says in order to please Him, whether any benefits return to them or not. One may not choose to do God's will in a *calculated* way.[11]

(8) *"Love is not easily irritated."*

The word here refers to *rousing to anger;* the basic idea behind it is "to sharpen." Sharp, pointed, spiked responses growing out of irritability do not readily flow from one who considers another's words and actions thoughtfully (i.e., lovingly). It is those who do not take the time to think through the situation and the words that they use in responding to it who sin in this respect. Again, they think about themselves. As we have seen throughout, so we see here again, the law of love means giving up our plans, our schedules, our ways, etc., in the interest of others'.

And it may extend to so seemingly a mundane matter as being sure to get enough sleep. Inadequate sleep leads to the temptation to respond in an irritable manner. Some persons who are constantly irritable, when put on a regular, eight-hour schedule find that the problem soon disappears. Sometimes, for the benefit of others, counselees must be willing to discipline themselves in their sleeping habits. But clearly, since sleep loss so fre-

---

10. Cf. my discussion of this term in *How to Overcome Evil* (Phillipsburg, N.J.: Presbyterian and Reformed, 1977), pp. 70ff.

11. Cf. my *What Do You Do When . . . ?* pamphlets in each of which this crucial point is made about the issue at hand.

quently leads to irritability, anyone working on the problem of irritability (or any other, for that matter), no matter what the occasion, should get regular sleep (and plenty of it) to create an atmosphere that is conducive to achieving good results. A sleep-starved person is exposing himself needlessly to temptation.

(9) *"Love doesn't keep records of wrongs."*

How often counselees do precisely what this law of love forbids: they count up, recall and throw up to another all the offenses that he has committed. Sometimes they actually keep writtens records!

Reading the phrase to a counselee from the *New Testament in Everyday English* (or *The Christian Counselor's New Testament*), with its literal translation, is one way to make the point. The fault is as clear an indication of the lack of love as any other. Forgiveness (in which one promises to remember the other's offenses against him no more, and then keeps his promise[12]) is the answer to this failure.

(10) *"Love isn't happy about injustice but happily stands on the side of truth."*

Love doesn't sit idly by when God's Word is attacked. It isn't mute about unfair actions against others. How often counselees need to take a stand for God, for righteousness, for truth (and for the ways of truth)! Often coward-ice — paralyzing concern over what others will do or say — is a clear sign of lack of love. Again, self-concern, rather than concern for one's neighbor, rears its unloving head. The solution to the problem is to get counselees to begin to take a stand for all that is right and against all that is wrong, wherever the lines may be drawn—regardless of the consequences to one's self. If there is no immediate issue to resolve, that beginning should take place at the counselee's next point of choice.

(11) *"Love covers all things."*

Here, in verse 7, we turn at last to four essential *positive* factors. The counselor will find himself pointing to them rather frequently. All four are

---

12. See my detailed and definitive discussion of forgiveness in *More than Redemption*, chapter 13.

rather broad in application (to each is appended the words "all things," or, possibly, "all sorts of things").

Rather than make a point of every offense against himself, as the unloving person does, the lover bears wrongdoing patiently. Indeed, out of love he even *covers* what has been done. He covers a *multitude* of sins. Now, this is not like the Watergate coverup, in which what ought to have been exposed was not (but instead, was covered with lies). Instead, it is the one who was wronged who covered the wrong with *love* (not with *lies*). It was not ignored, distorted, etc., but acknowledged—then covered in love (cf. I Pet. 4:8[13]). Not every wrong must be made an issue. Love doesn't allow these little rubs to come between believers. Instead, it covers these from his own eyes as well as from the eyes of all others.

(12) *"Love believes all things."*

True love, perhaps, is seen most clearly in the trust that it manifests in another. When others would doubt, the one who loves firmly believes. Only hard evidence[14] (never suspicion, general distrust or prejudice) would make him doubt another's word.

Surely this makes the lover vulnerable to others. When one lays his heart on the table, he invites others to run over it with track shoes. But love thinks first not of itself, but of others. That is why the lover is willing to run such risks. He would rather be injured himself than to injure another. The *disposition* of love always is to believe another if it is at all possible to do so. This quality is needed in counseling.

(13) *"Love hopes all things."*

Love always gives the other fellow the benefit of the doubt; it hopes for the best in another. It doesn't go around looking for what is wrong. This biblically realistic optimism doesn't grow out of faith in men, but in the God who can change them. So that, contrary to what so many counselees say ("He'll never do it; he never has before"), love says, "Perhaps this time

---

13. For more on this point, see my commentary on I Peter, *Trust and Obey* (Phillipsburg, N.J.: Presbyterian and Reformed, 1978).

14. Often this involves 2 or 3 witnesses. But even in the face of evidence, the lover always hears what the person has to say by way of explanation before condemning him (Prov. 18:17).

God will make him different.'' These two opposite attitudes tend to generate (or at least encourage) what they anticipate. And God (blessing His Word when it is obediently followed) may use the hopeful attitude in one person to stimulate change in another. Conversely, a spirit of hopelessness or resignation, when sensed by another, often provides further occasion for him to despair of change—even when he has been contemplating it.

(14) *"Love endures all things."*

Notice, again, in all four positive elements the words "all things" appear. There are no situations so bad that they allow an exception to what is said. All sorts of things can be covered, believed and hoped for in others when there is love. Similarly, we find in this phrase that every sort of offense, pressure, affliction and persecution can be endured in love. Because counselees so often deny the fact, claiming that their situation is unique—worse than anyone else's—the point in this verse must be stressed. All that is contained in I Corinthians 10:13 (see my exposition of that verse in my pamphlet, *Christ and Your Problems* [Phillipsburg, N.J.: Presbyterian and Reformed, 1971]) must be emphasized when helping a counselee. Basically there are three facts stressed in I Corinthians 10:13:

1. There are (at bottom) no unique problems;
2. But every problem is uniquely suited to the believer by God so that he can endure it (if he handles the problem God's way);
3. Every problem has a solution and will come to an end. Looking for the end helps one to endure it.

Counselees need both the hope and the responsibility that are spelled out by these two verses.

We have come to the close of section 2—the major emphasis of this discussion. One thing stands out (especially in contrast to vv. 1-3). The essentials of love outlined in verses 4 to 7 all boil down to this: love means putting others first. Every positive quality examined can only be destroyed by self-seeking; each can be enhanced by giving one's self more and more to others.

The route to love, therefore, is essentially the route to discipleship: to deny (crucify or put to death) the desires of self for Christ's sake, and then to follow Him by losing one's life for His sake and the gospel's (i.e., for God and others who will believe)—and (as a consequence; *not* as an end), thereby *finding* it. To love God and to love one's neighbor, indeed, does summarize the whole teaching of the Bible.

III. *Everlasting Aspects of Love* (vv. 8-13)

Prophecies, languages and knowledge (i.e., extraordinary revelatory prophecy—not mere preaching; extraordinary language capabilities—not normal human speech; and extraordinary discernment of God's ways and will—not the ordinary knowledge that comes from studying the Scriptures) will all come to an end.[15] But love will never fail (lit., "fall"—as a house falls into ruins).

Conclusion

Now, what can we learn about counseling from all of this? Much, much more than I can begin to describe. Let me therefore indicate just some general principles that (suggestively) may lead to other uses as well:

1. Clearly, Paul had more than the local *situation* in mind. He determined to meet their need for love in one area by teaching them (and us) all about love in general.[16]

2. Since counseling has to do with the relationship of counselees to God and to other persons, I Corinthians 13 is altogether pertinent to counselee problems. Of great significance in this regard is the fact that Jesus, when referring to the basic requirement in this twofold relationship, says that it is *love*.

---

15. Note: in v. 9, "languages" is omitted. When the completion of the N.T. takes place, special revelation and direction by prophecy and gifts of knowledge will be terminated. Languages, given to preach to unbelievers, will simply run out as the last missionary dies. In contrast, faith, hope and love will continue after these special gifts have disappeared.

The words used to describe how the other gifts "fall" are of significance: prophecies and knowledge will be "set aside" (*katargeo*="to cancel, destroy, do away with"), whereas languages (specially given) will "cease" (*pauo*="stop, come to an end"). The first two will be brought to an end, whereas tongues will cease.

16. Cf. Paul's general view of Scripture and its application that had it in mind when he wrote I Cor. (cf. 10:6, 11; 9:10). This expression precludes the idea of a *merely* local reference.

3. All that is said about love—in contrast to love*less* acts and states described in verses 1 to 3—has to do with others. The loveless life is the one that is focused and centered on one's self rather than on others. Even when one outwardly does something for another—to the extreme of giving his life—in a loveless way (to acquire fame and glory for himself, etc.), he is still self-centered.

Love moves out toward others, embracing them in attitude as well as act. Heart and hands, heart and lip agree.[17] Lovelessness moves inwardly toward one's self, ever seeking new ways to enhance and aggrandize the self—usually at the expense of others.

Thus, the same act—giving one's body to be burned, for instance— can be done in a loveless way (v. 3) or in a loving way (by standing for truth to help another; v. 6). That is one of the great lessons of the passage. That is the point that the Corinthians needed to learn as they used their gifts. Those gifts could be used lovingly or lovelessly. And that made all the difference.

4. Paul's description of love is a most useful source to which Christian counselors may turn—

a. to find descriptions of unloving attitudes and acts. The negative factors (4b-6a) are particularly helpful for this purpose. Often counselors must identify sinful behavior for their counselees for what it is (e.g., "That is an unmistakable instance of lovelessness that Paul here calls 'keeping records of wrongs,' John").

b. to find descriptions of loving acts and attitudes. Sometimes one counselee refuses to acknowlege that another is making progress. Here is one way to deal with that problem: "Mary, notice how he lovingly covered those rubs and didn't bring them up to you?"

c. to discover concrete counseling goals for which to shoot. Apart from such descriptions of love, it might seem to be an amorphous quality that is singularly elusive.

d. to give impetus to love by using these words to motivate counselees to please God.

---

17. Heart=the inner life we live before God and ourselves.

Much, much more could be said. Actual cases could be given in which each of these elements that we have discussed could be shown to bear on some counseling problem in one of the four ways just mentioned. But rather than do this for you, I suggest that you do the following as a practical exercise that will help prepare you for more effective counseling by learning how to use I Corinthians 13 in actual cases.

1. Purchase a copy of *The Christian Counselor's Casebook* (this volume contains 140 slices of actual cases).

2. Go through each case, using I Corinthians 13 for the four purposes just listed (a-d) wherever possible,[18] in one way or another bringing the principles and practices of the chapter to bear upon it.

3. Work out answers to the questions opposite each case selected, identifying the problems and solutions in terms of the biblical language and terminology that Paul uses in I Corinthians 13.

4. Wherever possible, develop concrete homework assignments (specifically adapted to each case) that grow out of and are appropriate to the principles of love described in I Corinthians 13.

Such an effort might be continued regularly, on a daily basis,[19] over a period of time until the principles of the chapter and their practical applications have been etched into your counseling practice. Few other efforts could be more rewarding.

---

18. Verses from I Cor. 13 will apply in almost every case since love (toward God and one's neighbor) is the sum of our whole duty before God.
19. Perhaps at the beginning of each daily study period.

7

Checks and Promptings

There is abroad today, in several forms, a teaching that has the potential to do much harm. It is motivated by a worthy desire to counter the intellectualizing of God's truth in ways that make that truth of little effect for Christian living. While no one can deny the desirability of achieving that goal, I find myself strongly opposing the proposals that this teaching offers as decidedly unscriptural and bound to cause much confusion among Christians.

The bare bones skeleton of the view amounts to this:

1. It is time that Christians stopped depending exclusively on truths handled by the intellect (and which stop there and go no further in influencing one's life style).

2. There is another way of obtaining direction from God—*through one's spirit*. This "spiritual truth," usually given in the form of "checks in one's spirit" (that forbid him to do something), or "promptings in his spirit" (impelling him to pursue various courses of action), is said to come *directly* from God as the Spirit contacts the believer's spirit.

3. One significant corollary of this teaching is that the Bible is not the sole source of divine revelation regarding life and godliness; another is that the Bible is not sufficient for guidance and decision making. Neither of these points is stated quite so flatly as I have expressed them; they are either denied (inconsistently) or reluctantly admitted only when one is driven against the wall by appropriate questioning.

Now, any number of observations may be made about those propositions. Let me make just one: There is no way in which one could ever discern either a "prompting" or a "check" in his spirit.

The spirit of a human being, on this view, is distinguished from his soul and from his body. The soul is said to be the receptor for rational proposi-

49

tional truth, which is perceived intellectually by it; the body is said to handle sense data from the material world. These sense data are discerned in some tangible form (felt, seen, smelled, heard, tasted). But "spiritual" promptings and checks are said to come some other way.

The question is, are such spiritual influences discerned? This is a serious question since neither the senses nor the mind is the perceiving agency. Spirit is invisible, intangible. If promptings and checks take neither a propositional nor a tangible form, what form do they take? How are they perceived? So far as I can see, there is no answer to this question; and none is given. What we can't know intellectually or organically we can't really know.[1]

But, of greater concern than the inherent anomalies is the warped view of guidance that it fosters. By it one is directed away from the sure Word of God (II Pet. 1:19). Instead, he is offered unidentifiable "checks" and "promptings" that are impossible to distinguish from feelings and notions generated by the person from within himself. That trade-off is no bargain.

But some persons, under the false notion that God must guide us when making decisions in a specific, detailed *ad hoc* manner rather than by specific and general principles of the Scriptures, actually do welcome the checks-and-promptings method as an advance over the historic Christian position. To them, there is probably little that I can say or do to dislodge them from such views; they are absolutely bent upon having God do all their detailed thinking for them—one wonders why He gave them either a brain or a Bible! It is amazing to think that the Holy Spirit spent thousands of years producing the Bible, then indwelt Christians for the purpose (among other things) of illuminating their understanding of the Scriptures, only to bypass the Bible and ignore the understanding by giving us unintelligible and intangible checks and promptings![2] They will persist in their ways until they

---

1. It is in this dilemma that the poverty of the triplex view of man which is basic to this teaching becomes so apparent. For a biblical consideration of the matter, see my *More than Redemption* (Phillipsburg, N.J.: Presbyterian and Reformed, 1979), pp. 108ff. In my opinion, one actually ends up interpreting his *feelings* as checks and promptings. But feelings are physiological phenomena.

2. The notion is impossible to conceive: checks and promptings would *have* to be intelligible to be *received and acted upon*.

50

begin to see that the checks and promptings with which they have been so enamored have led them up too many blind alleys or into circumstances that clearly show that the source of these negative and positive influences is not the Holy Spirit.

But to others, who are open to reading more deeply into the historic Christian position, let me refer you to the section of my book, *More than Redemption,* entitled "Personal Guidance" (pp. 22-34). In it, I have shown that a judicious and prayerful use of biblical principles, precepts and examples will yield everything that is needed to decide every question pertaining to life and godliness (II Pet. 1:3).

And, in addition, I wish to make a few observations about the biblical use of the word *spirit* that plainly prove one's spirit is not a separate, nonintellectual side of his human nature.

For starters, notice Acts 19:21, where we are told that "Paul decided in his spirit. . . ." The verb is *tithemi.* It is used with *kardia* ("heart") in Luke 21:14 as well as *pneuma* ("spirit") to mean that one has decided to do this *within himself.* The two expressions mean that something is thought through and determined in one's mind. And notice, especially—this is the point of significance to us—what happens *in the spirit* is decidedly *intellectual:* a determination, a decision, is made. Surely the spirit is conceived of as operating rationally, intellectually.

In Ephesians 4:23, Paul writes of being "renewed in the spirit of your mind." If the word "spirit" here refers to the human spirit, the verse somehow combines this spirit with the mind (*nous*): the spirit is said either (1) to be within, or a part of the mind, or (2) to be composed of mind. However, it is also possible to take the word *spirit* to refer to the Holy Spirit and to interpret the passage as meaning "renewed by the Spirit who works on (or in) your mind." Taking the passage this way, we see that the Spirit works not in some non-intellectual area called the spirit, but in the mind—i.e., He renews us intellectually so that we begin to think God's thoughts after Him (cf. Col. 3:10; Isa. 55:7-9). Probably "spirit" here means attitude: "rejuvenated in your mental attitude," and has nothing to do with the question.

It is not surprising, then, that one is given a "spirit of wisdom of revelation and of full knowledge" (Eph. 1:17) in answer to prayer. Since the spirit is being renewed in knowledge and holiness, it will grow in its ability to make wise choices based upon its accumulation of knowledge. But, once more, don't fail to note the intellectual commodities in which the human spirit traffics.

In its quest for answers, the spirit searches (Ps. 77:6). This search, incidentally, is described in Hebrew synonymous poetic parallelism (i.e., where adjoining lines say the same thing in different words) as identical to *speaking in one's own heart*. It clearly portrays inner intellectual dialog within one's self (cf. Job 20:2, and, especially, Job 32:8; note too Job 32:18). This inner source of thought and decision can be sinful so that the spirit must be cleansed from defilement (II Cor. 7:1), and false prophets may prophesy ''out of their own heart'' and ''after their own spirit'' (Ezek. 13:2, 3). Incidentally, here again, as in many places in the Bible, heart and spirit are used synonymously to refer to the inner life. And when Paul says that the Spirit ''testifies'' (an intellectual term) with (*sun*=''together with''; not ''to'' our spirit) ''our spirit that we are God's children,'' don't fail to note that there is specific, rational, propositional content to that testimony. And, even when some in Corinth attempted to become involved in some sort of ecstatic enthusiasm by which they sought to divorce spiritual influences from the intellect, they were forbidden to do so (cf. I Cor. 14:15, 16). And we are expressly informed that one's spirit is under our intelligent control (I Cor. 14:32).

So, it seems perfectly clear that the check-and-prompting view fails to take into account the biblical evidence. Indeed, it has no biblical warrant at all. The teaching is based on experience (wrongly interpreted) and not on exegesis.

But of what importance is all this to biblical counselors? It has a number of implications for counseling. Here are three:

1. Counselors must be careful about how they speak to counselees; they dare not use language that might be misinterpreted to approve of the checks and promptings view.

2. Counselors must be clear in their own minds about the proper biblical view of guidance.

3. Counselors must begin to look for the effects of this erroneous doctrine in

52

the lives of counselees. It can lie beneath confusion, behind discouragement or at the base of doubt. Since the view is spreading rapidly, the incidences of counselee difficulty stemming from it doubtlless will be on the increase in the near future. It is important to look ahead and to anticipate problems so that we may be alert to them and prepared to meet them as often as we can.

8
Does the Behaviorist Have a Mind?

In the Volume XXV, Number 1 (January, 1927) issue of *The Princeton Theological Review,* there appeared an article by Prof. Wm. Hallock Johnson entitled "Does the Behaviorist Have a Mind?"

This article, buried among musty periodicals on library shelves, has long since been forgotten. In those early days of behaviorism, though Johnson saw its dangers, few others believed that such a view as Watson's had a chance. We who live some 50 years later see that it has in many ways achieved its purpose.

Of course, the work of B. F. Skinner (who inherited Watson's mantle) was not on the scene as a threat at the time when Johnson wrote. But Johnson took on John B. Watson, the leading exponent in his day. It is interesting to note that if you strip Skinner of his more precise instrumentation, you find Watson beneath the modern clothing. Peeled down to the basics, Johnson, therefore, meets not only Watson but Skinner as well.

The old article is worth exhuming and preserving. In contrast to much evangelical capitulation to behaviorism, it still constitutes an "update on Christian counseling." We have reprinted it in full.

DOES THE BEHAVIORIST HAVE A MIND?

There is a good deal to be said on both sides of this question. The behaviorist himself assures us that he, or at least the subject of his investigations (for he disclaims introspection), has no mind, no instincts, no will or purpose, in fact no consciousness at all as distinct from bodily reaction to physical stimuli. Stimulus and response tell the whole story, and the response is always of the type of congenital or conditioned reflex action. If the behaviorist should be conscious of his reflex actions, he would be acting out of character and would be false to his professed principles. His own answer to the question of our title is in the negative. He does not claim to have a mind, he will not admit that he has a mind as distinguished from the body, and if the stimulus of the question, "Do you have a mind?" should be presented to him, the response to be expected would be an indignant and emphatic, "No."

There is, however, another side to the question. The behaviorist in spite of his protestations certainly acts as if he had a mind. His pursuits are wholly in the intellectual realm. His main business is nothing else than writing books and articles for learned magazines, conducting experiments which demand some mental equipment to estimate their bearing and value, teaching the young idea that there are no such things as ideas, and instructing classes of other minds that there are no minds at all. The behaviorist uses all the weapons in the arsenal of debate, ridicule, assumption of superior intelligence and learning, and calling of names such as "medievalist" and "mystic." His aim, it is true (although he admits no such thing as purpose), is to convert people to his way of thinking and to affect the thinking processes of the scholastic world in such a way as to bring them all to the opinion that there is no mind; but his manner of doing this is that of the "high brow" and the intellectual. He is incurably intellectual even when he vilifies the faculty of reason which is the candle of the Lord within us.

Both sides in the discussion should be aware of the fact that the case is so foolish and so absurd on the face of it that it is in danger of being thrown out of court. The behaviorist who maintains that he has no mind cannot help refuting himself every time he utters a word, or frames an argument, or puts pen to paper. The defender of the affirmative on the other hand—who maintains that the behaviorist has a mind—is placed in the uncomfortable position of one who can simply vociferate the obvious. He cannot use effectively the method of *reductio ad absurdum* because nothing in his view can be more absurd than the position with which the behaviorist begins. He can apparently do little more than ring the changes upon the characterizations, "glaringly inconsistent" and "palpably absurd."

A university president in the Midwest recently said that in taking up administrative duties he was compelled to commit intellectual suicide, and another president in the East admitted that he had become a "talking machine." If the personalities of these two presidents should be merged into one—if the intellectual suicide should be turned into a talking machine—it is to be feared that the resulting utterances would not be very significant. The behaviorist is a kind of dual personality. On the one hand he claims (or admits) that he has no mind or will or purpose, but on the other hand he says that "the interest of the behaviorist in man's doings is more than the interest of the spectator—he wants to control man's reactions as physical scientists want to control and manipulate other natural phenomena."[1] As a behaviorist he has no mind of his own and no purpose of his own and as a strict determinist he cannot control his own conduct, but in his efforts to reduce psychology to a natural science he wishes to control and predict the conduct of everybody else. There must be a contradiction here somewhere. The behaviorist cannot play both roles at once. But if there is an inescapable contradiction or mental twist in the behaviorist's mind in his fundamental assumption that " 'consciousness' is neither a definable nor a usable concept,"[2] we fear that there may be a moral twist in the kind of conduct he wishes to produce and control. If the behaviorist should be allowed full sway in regulating conduct, we fear that the result would be thoughtless activity, and meaningless behavior, and conscienceless conduct.

Psychology is no longer merely an academic discipline fitted to provide pleasant mental exercise for the classroom. It has entered our homes and our business as well as out schools, and has invaded the realms of ethics, jurisprudence and religion. The salesman in approaching his prospect or seeking to become a super-salesman, the corporation executive in selecting his personnel and in promoting efficiency, the advertiser in attracting the public, the struggling clerk aspiring to the presidency of his concern, the statesman who would prevent war and the reformer who would repress crime, the young man in search of a wife and the mother anxious for the upbringing of her children—all are invited to sit at the feet of the psychologist. The educator with his methods and projects and programs of study is

1. John B. Watson, *Behaviorism*, p. 11.
2. P. 3.

peculiarly at the mercy of the psychologist, and the church is beginning to realize that her whole program of religious education may, for good or evil, be profoundly modified under the influence of popular psychological theory. As a thoughtful student of the subject has said: "In the new educational enterprises of the church a matter of utmost concern is the selection of a psychological basis on which the new program is to stand. A choice between the schools has to do with something more important than methods and materials. It has to do with the maintenance or the abandonment of certain elements of the Christian religion which have heretofore been considered essential."[3]

When the behaviorist seeks by logical argument to abolish logic, and from his platform of mechanistic determinism announces his ambition to control the thought and conduct of the world, we are tempted to attribute his inconsistencies to mental obtuseness or perversity, and following the advice of the wise man to "answer a fool according to his folly." This, however, is not to deny that the behaviorist in his experiments has made contributions of value to psychological science, or that in spite of his disclaimer of introspection he has sometimes shown a shrewd and penetrating insight into human nature.

It will prove instructive to glance at the newest book in the field of psychology, *Psychologies of 1925,* containing lectures given at Clark University in 1925 and in the early months of 1926 by leading psychologists. Their names in alphabetical order are Madison Bentley, Knight Dunlap, Walter S. Hunter, Kurt Koffka, Wolfgang Köhler, Morton Prince, William McDougall, John B. Watson, and Robert S. Woodworth. McDougall of Harvard tells us that the mechanists in psychology would have us believe that men are "robots," this name being applied in a recent play to ingeniously constructed machines in the shape of human beings. McDougall adds that "the view that men are merely such robots is now being dogmatically taught to thousands of young students in the psychological departments of the universities of this country."[4] He finds that this view is now enjoying an alarming popularity, and that the spread of this way of thinking among

---

3. W. A. Squires, *Psychological Foundations of Religious Education,* pp. 30, 31.
4. P. 275.

psychologists has gone so far that those who do not accept it are regarded as "cranky persons wedded to medieval metaphysics" and as "queer survivors from the dark ages," incapable of joining in the triumphant march of modern science. The behaviorists may be robots in whom reflex action takes the place formerly assigned to reflection, but they are sure that their reflexes are right and that the reflexes of others, the upholders of rival theories, are wrong. They differ also from the real robots in the fact that, as we have seen, they have far-reaching and revolutionary plans for the application of their doctrine not only in the sphere of psychology but in the fields of education, philosophy, ethics and jurisprudence. Look first at the application in the realm of philosophy. Holding that all the objects in our environment are ultimately electric charges, W. S. Hunter adds that "so likewise is the human animal and the aggregations of human animals which make up society. If the phenomenon of a storage battery is a matter of electrons and protons, so is the phenomenon of family life."[5] Hunter is naturally indignant with the older psychological method "which is inseparably bound up with the ancient philosophical concepts of mind and consciousness as aspects of the universe which differ from the physical."[6]

John B. Watson, the recognized leader of the behaviorist group, finds a "mystical" element even in Hunter's exposition. He is uncompromising in his purpose to rule mind and consciousness out of the picture, and in the interest of behaviorism would revise ethics and jurisprudence, and would apparently do away with the church and religion altogether. It would be interesting to see what kind of a code of ethics the new "experimental ethics" of behaviorism (which Watson admits does not yet exist) would formulate. It would be still more interesting to discover the kind of behavior in the moral sphere in which the principles of behaviorism when freely carried out actually eventuate. Watson would like to make some profound changes in the field of jurisprudence. He would do away with punishment in the rearing of children and the treatment of criminals. He tells us that "punishment is a word which never ought to have crept into our language"[7]

---

5. P. 90.
6. P. 107.
7. P. 71.

—which raises the question whether the man who first introduced it ought not to have been punished. Watson is at pains to emphasize the fact that "the behaviorist is a strict determinist."[8] It follows then, as he declares in italics, that "the child or adult has to do what he does. The only way he can be made to act differently is first to untrain him and then retrain him." Naturally the untraining and retraining must be done by the behaviorist; the other people or psychologists of other schools have no power to retrain the behaviorist. There are of course no criminals in the usual sense of persons who have committed acts that deserve punishment. There are only "deviants," and these are of two kinds, the insane and the "socially untrained." The insane should be sent to the asylum and the socially untrained should be sent to school. We may remark here that even Watson has not been able wholly to emancipate himself from the ideas of free-will, responsibility and desert, so deeply imbedded in our thought and our vocabulary. He will allow a gentle rap on the knuckles of the child if promptly adminstered; and if the socially untrained deviants through obtuseness or obstinacy refuse to take on the training that will fit them to re-enter society, he would even for "ten to fifteen years or even longer" make them "earn their daily bread, in vast manufacturing and agricultural institutions, escape from which is impossible."[9] "Strenuous work sixteen hours per day," Watson naively adds, "will hurt no one." Of course, it is insisted that the care of such deviants should be in the hands of behaviorists. Such a reform in criminal jurisprudence, Watson admits, is only a pious dream "until all the lawyers and jurists decide to become behaviorists." Now since every lawyer and jurist together with every other adult "has to do what he does," what probability is there that any lawyer or judge will "decide" to change his mind and act differently? The only way to reform the lawyers and jurists is to put them where they deserve to be, in a "school" (not a prison of course for this would savor too much of the "religious theory" of retaliation) where they could be restrained and made to work for sixteen hours a day, until under the gentle tutelage of behaviorist wardens they come to see the error of their ways and give evidence of true repentance for doing what they couldn't help doing. Like other mechanical determinists who would do away with the guilt

8. P. 71.
9. Pp. 71-74.

or fault or responsibility of the offender against society, Watson can only transfer these notions of guilt and responsibility from the criminal to his social environment. It is our own "fault," he says, that is, the fault of parents, teachers and others of the group, if individuals "go wrong" or deviate from set standards of behavior.

If the insane should be placed in asylums and the socially untrained in schools, how can we tell which is which? If it be found that an alleged criminal does not know what he is doing, how does he differ from anyone else? If he does know what he is doing, then there is something—knowledge or awareness or consciousness—that is of a non-material character and is distinct from, and over and above, his bodily action. Again, how can the behaviorist distinguish between the socially trained and the socially untrained? Let us suppose that a gun is discharged and a person is killed. How is the behaviorist, who denies that purpose influences behavior, to distinguish between accidental homicide and deliberate murder? The whole question, as Prince points out, is whether there is "criminal intent," and the question is unanswerable on behaviorist principles. Carl Murchison, the editor of the volume, makes a point as old as the reply of Zeno to his thieving slave when he insists elsewhere that a philosophy of rigid determinism "is sheer nonsense when applied only to the individual offender and not also to the community which contains him. If it has been determined by circumstances that an individual commits a crime, let it also be determined by circumstances that a social community will strike back with sure and swift punishment."

Before going further it may be worthwhile to glance at the historical antecedents of behaviorism and at the criticism which it directs against other psychological schools, and then we may look a little more in detail at the objections which may be made against behaviorism itself.

In taking up the book of Clark University lectures we are bewildered by the present variety of conflicting theories in the psychological field. We find here represented Schools of Behaviorism, Dynamic Psychology, Gestalt, Purposive Groups, Reaction Psychology, and Psychologies called Structural. One lecturer, Knight Dunlap, says: "The announcement of a new book on *The new psychology and the preacher* might, so far as anyone could predict in advance, be a treatise based on the Freudian or some other

60

psychoanalytic system; it might be an exposition of 'new thought' or some other vagary of the Quimby brood; it might be an application of the theories and methods of 'intelligence testing'; it might be propaganda for the theories and practices of M. Coué; it might be one of the numerous embodiments of phrenology under its more recent name of 'character analysis'; it might be a book on psychic research concerning spooks and other magical notions; or it might be one of the less easily nameable nostrums which strut before the public in borrowed plumage, calling themselves 'the new psychology.' "[10] Dunlap himself, in contrast to the host of pseudopsychologists and to the older "Malebranchian psychology," is an exponent of "scientific psychology" which does away with the superstition that "mind" is "distinct from, but miraculously related to the body."[11]

In tracing the pedigree of behaviorism we find that in the past generation at least four different schools of psychology, each of them associated with some movement in science or philosophy, have successively held the field. There was first the psychology of the soul, and this soul had "faculties" such as memory, imagination, will and so forth. It was then objected that the assumption of a soul was unnecessary for purposes of science and that the separate faculties were abstractions, and it was maintained that the proper study of the psychologist was consciousness, or conscious states or processes in more or less close association with brain concomitants. The soul according to James had "worn out both itself and its welcome," and according to Wundt it was "a metaphysical surplusage for which psychology has no use." Later there arose the functional psychology, studying the mind or consciousness as a servant of the organism and as a means of adjustment of the organism to its environment. Finally the behaviorist, denying the utility of introspection, banished consciousness entirely from the psychological field or reduced it to a name for the relation between the nervous system and its stimulating environment. We may remind ourselves that the psychology of consciousness and its processes (or of ideas and their associations) was stimulated by the growing knowledge of brain physiology, and its philosophical background was the traditional English empiricism coming down from Locke and Hume. The functional psychology was an

---

10. P. 309.
11. P. 312.

application of popular biological categories to the study of mind, and it was associated with the pragmatic movement in philosophy. Behaviorism was an outgrowth of the study of animal behavior, and its philosophical affinities are with eighteenth century materialism and with the New Realism which in its revolt from subjective idealism would define consciousness as a name for the relation between the object and the nervous system.

Behaviorism is a sort of "psychological materialism," to borrow a phrase from Dr. Patton's recent volume. It first dismisses the consciousness of animals and then of human beings as inaccessible to knowledge, and holds that when we attempt to peer into the secrets of our own "minds" all we discover is a feeling of flexed muscles, of visceral movements, and of laryngeal movements associated with spoken language or "silent" language. Consciousness as something distinct from bodily movement does not exist. It is either a myth or is only another name for the relation between the bodily organism and the physical stimulus. Plainly behaviorism is directly opposed to the fundamental convictions of religion, that there is a spirit in man and that the inspiration of the Almighty giveth them understanding, and that there will be a conscious existence of the individual after the death of the body.

A characteristic of behaviorism is the boldness of its negations and the thoroughness with which it disposes of the spiritual or non-material element in man. The soul with its faculties, the mind with its categories, the will with its purposes and freedom, consciousness with its processes and concomitant brain process, ideas with their associations, and even the instincts with their evolution are all thrown upon the scrap-heap. Behaviorism has not only cleaned house but has moved out of its house. One behaviorist, Hunter, would give over the term psychology to the exponents of antiquated methods, while coining the term "anthroponomy" to describe behaviorism or the "science of human behavior."[12] We recall the witty criticism directed against Hume, that he went outside his house and looked in at the window and could find no one at home. The behaviorist has not only gone outside his house, but has closed the shutters and moved away.

The defender of spiritual realities and values will find something instruc-

___
12. P. 83.

tive in the behaviorist's critique of his predecessors and rivals in the psychological field. The same methods by which the psychology of ideas or of consciousness disposed of the soul as a spiritual entity are adopted by the behaviorist in disposing of ideas and consciousness altogether. If the soul was inaccessible to knowledge, so also is the mind or consciousness as a separate entity. If the old-fashioned faculties and functions were abstractions or myths, so also are the more modern ideas and their associations. The weapons used by the psychology-without-a-soul are now turned against itself by the psychology-without-a-mind. Watson insists that consciousness is "merely another word for the 'soul' of more ancient times," and that the metaphysical implications of the two terms are identical.[13] Behaviorism is in fact psychology without a soul reduced to absurdity.

It is interesting and somewhat comforting to notice further that some popular and ultra-modern theories which have been regarded as hostile to a religious view of things are by behaviorism buried as deep as the old soul-psychology. Empiricism with its exploiting of impersonal ideas, physiological psychology with its concomitance of conscious process and brain process, epiphenomenism which treated mind as a fly-wheel of matter, psychophysical parallelism which chained mind to matter without allowing it any influence upon the movements of matter, Freudian psychoanalysis which substituted the unconscious wish for the "will that can," and even evolutionary ideas of mind which assimilated the mind of man to that of the brute, are all junked without ceremony to make way for the up to date machinery of behaviorism.

The behavioristic materialist takes a short method with the spiritualist. He rightly fears that consciousness even if cast in the modest role of epiphenomenon may by some ingenious turn assume the leading role. The only safe way is to exclude it from the cast altogether. Consciousness may start the voyage as a stowaway in the cargo of mechanism, but there is always danger that it may mutiny and take command of the ship. Consciousness may be tied securely to brain process, but Bergson may be right when he says that conscious activity overflows brain activity on all sides. Consciousness may be merely an instrument of adaptation in the struggle for existence, but in the end the servant may become the master and the development of mind

13. *Behaviorism*, pp. 3, 5.

and freedom may be seen as the end of the whole process. The only safe way for the mechanical behaviorist is to exclude altogether this uncomfortable and dangerous intruder, consciousness. "Nowhere is it necessary to introduce the concept of consciousness, or experience, conceived as another mode of existence, or as another aspect of the physical world."[14] Of course the intelligence tests will have to go, for there is no such thing as intelligence; and it is to be hoped that the reactions to the College Entrance Board examinations now demanded of young students will be greatly simplified.

The behaviorist has to do his fighting on two fronts. On one front are the introspectionists, the purposivists, and the metaphysical and theological opponents of materialism; but on the other front he finds arrayed against him the popular evolutionary and psycho-analytical schools. Watson is contemptuous of all that has been written about the evolution of instinct and the classification of instincts. Instinct is defined as "a combination of congenital responses unfolding serially under appropriate stimulation." What we call instincts are for the most part "learned" or "conditioned" reflexes. Going as he admits beyond the evidence, Watson holds that there is no inheritance of mental traits or aptitudes, and he makes training and environment all-powerful. Human beings of all geological ages, of all races and conditions have the same set of unlearned responses—"be it in Africa or in Boston, be it in the year six million B.C. or in 1925 A.D."[15]—and these responses are due to the material out of which men are made and the way this is put together. Most of the treatises on instinct have been written by the "armchair" psychologists who have not studied the behavior of young animals or babies from birth. The Darwinian geneticists "are working under the banner of the old 'faculty' psychology."[16] In fact the whole concept of instinct has become "academic and meaningless," and "actual observation thus makes it impossible for us any longer to entertain the concept of instinct."[17]

The behaviorists and the Freudians were quite friendly ten years ago, but now no love is lost between the two schools. Psychoanalysis is in fact

---

14. Hunter, p. 104.
15. P. 3.
16. P. 6.
17. P. 32.

introspectionism and introspectionism raised to the *n*th degree. The Freudian delves into the mysteries not only of consciousness but of the subconscious and the unconscious. He deals with dreams, with suppressed wishes, and with unconscious complexes. He is naturally *persona non grata* with the behaviorist, and the Freudian emotions go the way of the evolutionary instincts. The elaborate writings of the Freudians, enough in the past twenty years we are told to fill a good-sized room,[18] are consigned by Watson to the waste basket.

"The history of modern philosophy," says Will Durant in his *Story of Philosophy*, "might be written in terms of the warfare of physics and psychology." But in recent times these two antagonists seem to have changed sides. The physicists have been spiritualizing matter, interpreting it in terms of energy and even of will, while the psychologists have been busy in banishing the soul and spirit and even consciousness and purpose from the universe. President Butler of Columbia University has said that "psychology has demonstrated its capacity to become both frivolous and inconsequent"; and in his latest annual report he maintains that "The new and numerous Philistines are the proud discoverers and professors of a new doctrine of behavior which finds nothing to behave and no purpose in behaving. Where they have touched education they are reducing it to a costly pantomime." But perhaps we ought to distinguish between varieties or schools of behaviorism. McDougall distingishes three schools, the Strict Behaviorists, the Purposive Behaviorists, and the Near Behaviorists. We are not concerned with the purposive behaviorists, although it must be recognized that some psychologists can use the term "purpose" as if it were something inherent in the object rather than the subject. E. C. Tolman, a purposive behaviorist, is careful to state that his own doctrine is "not a mere Muscle Twitchism of the Watsonian variety."[19] If the strict behaviorists may be called muscle twitchers the near behaviorists should be termed "steam whistlers." Thus Morton Prince (in the volume of lectures before us) reminds us that Huxley as long as fifty years ago spoke of consciousness in brutes and then in men as only a collateral product of the working of the bodily mechanism, and "as completely without the power of modifying that

18. P. 37.
19. P. 279n.

65

working as the steam whistle, which accompanies the work of a locomotive engine, is without influence upon its machinery."[20]

The near behaviorists do not deny that consciousness exists, but adopting the Huxleyan automatism they have as little to do with consciousness as possible and do not allow it to do anything. The strict behaviorists, of whom Watson is the principal spokesman, do away with mind or consciousness altogether. Watson will not admit that mental states exist and he says that behaviorism ignores them just as chemistry ignores alchemy. "The behaviorist does not concern himself with them because as the stream of his science broadens and deepens such older concepts are sucked under, never to reappear."

By his assumption that there is no such thing as mind or consciousness the behaviorist has thrown out a protective mechanism that is impervious to the weapons alike of argument and of ridicule. When he reduces instincts to the congenital responses of fear, love, anger, etc. (he apologizes for the continued use of these "literary" terms), or to love behavior, rage behavior and fear behavior, it is useless to point out to him that there is a conscious content in these primary responses and a great gulf fixed between them and purely mechanical action. When Watson says again: "By 'memory,' then, we mean nothing except the fact that when we meet a stimulus again after an absence, we do the old habitual thing—that we learned to do when we were in the presence of that stimulus in the first place,"[21] we would waste our breath if we insisted that we could never recognize the stimulus as the same nor the response as the same without the aid of the discarded memory. And when, further, responses and reflexes are substituted for purpose it is idle to declare, using the words of John Dewey, that "complete adaptation to environment means death. The essential point in all response is the desire to control the environment." The trenchant arguments of J. B. Pratt in his *Matter and Spirit,* of Lovejoy in his "Paradox of the Thinking Behaviorist,"[22] and of McDougall and Prince in the volume we have been considering seem to make no dent in the behaviorist's armor. Perhaps our

20. P. 200.
21. *Behaviorism,* p. 190.
22. *Philosophical Review,* March, 1922.

only refuge is in the hope that you can't fool all the people—even all the psychologists—all the time.

Possibly we may find a vulnerable point in one of Watson's favorite illustrations, used in his lectures in *Psychologies of 1925* and his *Behaviorism* (1925), for the purpose of proving that "psychology is a natural science—a definite part of biology."[23] "I have in my hand a hardwood stick. If I throw it forward and upward it goes a certain distance and drops to the ground. I retrieve the stick, put it in hot water, bend it at a certain angle, throw it out again—it goes outward, revolving as it goes for a short distance, turns to the right then drops down. Again I retrieve the stick, reshape it slightly and make its edges convex. I call it a boomerang. Again I throw it upward and outward. Again it goes forward revolving as it goes. Suddenly it turns, comes back and gracefully and kindly falls at my feet. It is still a stick, still made of the same material, but it has been shaped differently. *Has the boomerang an instinct to return to the hand of the thrower?* No? Well, why does it return? Because it is made in such a manner that when it is thrown upward and outward with a given force it must return (parallelogram of forces)."[24] The application is obvious. "Man is made up of certain kinds of material—put together in certain ways. If he is hurled into action (as a result of stimulation) may he not exhibit movement (in advance of training) just as peculiar as (but no more mysterious than) that of the boomerang?"[25]

Sometimes the boomerang returns to smite the thrower. The two objects compared, boomerang and man, differ in several essential respects. The man knows what he is doing when he makes the boomerang, and he makes it for a special purpose, so that something beside the boomerang illustration is needed to banish consciousness and purpose from the universe. Perhaps the mechanical action of the boomerang will illustrate action of the simple reflex type, but even this is doubtful. Kurt Koffka says that "Marina dissected the inner and outer muscles of monkeys and connected them crossways. An impulse sent to contract the external muscle of the right eye ought now to result in a movement toward the left and vice versa. The monkey should look to the left when a bright spot appears at the right. In reality, nothing of the kind took place. As soon as the wounds healed the animal moved his eyes as

---

23. See p. 34 of the former volume, from which we quote.
24. Pp. 12, 13.
25. P. 13.

67

normally as before the operation. Thus the conception of a merely contingent connection between situation and response breaks down even at the reflex level."[26]

It is fortunate that the boomerang cannot "deviate" or be guilty of "socially untrained" conduct, but this emphasizes the fact that it cannot be trained to make "learned" or "conditioned" responses. What a world of mental activity in both learner and teacher may be concealed under the term "learned responses"! Why cannot the boomerang learn? Another difference, and one that opens the gap between man and boomerang still wider, is that a man, if he is a behaviorist, can alter or condition the actions of people, if he can catch them young enough, to an indefinite extent. If the behaviorist had his way with children the babies would stop crying (except when in actual pain) and would no longer be frightened by black cats or other animals, the preachers would stop preaching, the introspectionists would stop introspecting, the judges would leave the bench, psychology would become "a natural science," and everybody would be happy. It is a paradox that people who insist upon putting on others the strait jacket of "strict determinism" reserve for themselves the liberty of influencing the thoughts and conduct of their fellows in a way that almost approaches omnipotence. When it comes to pass that boomerangs begin to instruct and reform their fellow boomerangs and teach them to deviate from the path of "congenital response," then the analogy between boomerang and man, between boomerang and behaviorist, will be more convincing.

Another striking fact, not to overdo the matter, is that a boomerang cannot talk. We strongly suspect that man is a talking animal because he is a thinking animal, and we recall the statement of Max Müller to the effect that "the formation of language attests from the very first the presence of a rational mind." To be on safe ground the behaviorist should stop talking and, as one of his critics advises, "content himself with relaxing and contracting his muscles." As soon as the behaviorist (even if it be in Carnegie Hall at two or three dollars per ticket) begins to debate the question, "Is Man a Machine?" he *ipso facto* ceases to be a machine. He should not only stop talking, but should stop being conscious that he is

---

26. P. 131.

68

stopping. The only consistent behaviorist is the behaviorist when he is asleep and not dreaming.

We suspect that what the behaviorist has in mind when he denies the existence of mind or consciousness is an objection not so much to the existence as to the efficiency of consciousness. With proper scorn and in italics Watson remarks that "'no psychologist today would like to be classed as believing in *interaction.—If 'mind' acts on body, then all physical laws are invalid.*"[27] The editor of the Clark University volume, Carl Murchison, shrewdly remarks that he is convinced "that experimental methods are largely instances of the more or less systematic theories of the experimenter." The shortcomings of the behavioristic psychologists are due to the philosophy of materialism and mechanism which underlies their psychology. It is this that leads them sedulously to avoid "anthropomorphism" even when dealing with human nature, and to side-track at all costs the problems of knowledge, of purpose and of the psychophysical relation.

Consciousness—that is, efficient consciousness—is the Great Intruder in a mechanical or naturalistic scheme of the universe. At all costs it must be kept from doing anything, and the only safe way to keep it from doing anything is to exclude it from real existence altogether. Huxley's "steam whistle" theory was only partially satisfactory, and the theory of parallelism, which was popular twenty years ago but is now rather *démodé*, while it effectually side-tracked consciousness and kept it from any influence upon events in the physical world, at least allowed to it a quasi-activity in its own sphere. The method of the modern psychologist is more drastic. He ignores the very existence of consciousness. In haughty disdain he passes it by without recognition. If compelled to notice it at all he at once merges it into the organism on the one hand or the environment on the other. If a behaviorist of the Watson school, he identifies it with bodily movement, especially laryngeal vibration. If an evolutionist of the Dewey school, he characterizes it as a quality of the "real object." The same motives that induce the naturalistic theologian to deny miracle and the supernatural, so as to shut out the activity of a personal God from nature, history and experience, operate with the naturalistic philosopher or psychologist and lead him to exclude an efficient consciousness from his scheme of things altogether.

---

27. *Behaviorism*, pp. 242, 243.

The result is what may be called an intellectual apostasy in our intellectual centers and our great universities. The intellect in circles in which it should magnify its office, that is in the departments of philosophy and psychology in our universities, sees fit to abdicate its throne, and to immolate itself upon the altar of materialism and mechanism. The young people in our schools are forbidden to believe in that essential quality of human nature which distinguishes man from the brute. They are forbidden to look backward in memory, or inward in introspection and self-examination, or forward in purpose, or upward in worship. They are asked to accept a philosophy which makes the philosopher (to borrow a phrase from Durant's *Story of Philosophy*) "an automaton automatically reflecting upon his own automatism."

After all the strongest indictment against behaviorism is not that it is hopelessly inconsistent and palpably absurd but that it obliterates all moral distinctions. What sort of behavior will behaviorism legitimately promote? This is the most important question when multitudes of the youth in our colleges and universities are being taught its principles. The plain fact is that morality as a binding restraint upon human conduct and with it reverence for life and the sacredness of human personality are by the progress of behaviorism "sucked under, never to reappear." If the conduct of man is first assimilated to that of the animal, and then the behavior of both animal and man is further reduced by a rigid determinism to the type of mechanical action, if unsocial conduct is simply that which the majority dislikes, although a more enlightened minority may think it desirable for its purpose, then the safeguards thrown by morality and religion around human life and the family relation and the obligations of law and the rights of property are broken down. Then the legitimate fruit of behaviorism in the sphere of moral behavior is indicated by the statement of one of the principles in a famous murder case, that it is as justifiable to kill a human being for the purposes of science as to stick a pin through a beetle.

What is needed today is, to use an expression of the late Professor Ormond, the "re-ification of the Ego." When consciousness goes conscience goes with it, and when free-will and responsibility are denied their place is taken by lawless individualism and an ethic of self-assertion.

Lincoln University, Pa.   WM. HALLOCK JOHNSON.

9

Eclecticism in Counseling

For some time, in various places, I have been trying to expose and counter the prevailing spirit of eclecticism in counseling that exists among Bible-believing persons. I have been (and am) concerned about this because, in my opinion, the battle with eclecticism is the most important struggle in which we may engage today. And that struggle *must* be won. Perhaps it is time, therefore, to extend the discussion just a bit.

But first, you may wish to inquire, "How is the battle going?" I would say in some sectors quite well; in others, not so well.

Among ministers and key Christian laymen, in general, there has been a significant awakening to the problem together with a clearly discernible trend to solve that problem. Literally thousands upon thousands of Christians have become articulately aware of the inroads of eclecticism and are combining their forces to sweep it out of their churches and church institutions. This is encouraging, but even more gratifying than this necessary negative effort is the evidence that most of these persons are engaged in strong positive endeavors to learn to do biblical counseling instead.

The battle has gone poorly (with some notable exceptions) in the teaching institutions. Here among vested interests in centers and strongholds of eclectic thought, professionalism, as well as other factors, has hindered advance. Then, too, it should be remembered, nouthetic leaders have had their hands so full helping out the sergeants and the troops on the front lines that they have not yet spent much time trying to influence the generals back at home. But the time has now come when that defect must be remedied. There are capable men within the movement who are concerned to work at this and who (indeed) have begun to do so already. Many more are now preparing for it by means of graduate studies recently introduced at the Christian Counseling and Educational Center in Philadelphia.[1]

But, now, let us consider the origin of this strange word, eclecticism. The term comes from a Greek word *eklego* (which itself is a combination of *legein,* "to gather" and *ek,* "out" = "to gather out"), which means "to pick out," or (as we ourselves say in English) "to pick and choose." The Greek "eclectics" were philosophers who belonged to no particular school. Instead, they took bits and pieces from various sources and glued them together. As we know him today, an eclectic is one who makes a patchwork quilt of counseling theory and practice, taking from various schools what seems best to him. We could say that the principle of eclecticism is:

Each counselor himself is the measure of what is best (or right).

But, in this sense, the word *eclectic* does not appear in the New Testament.

Nevertheless, the *idea* of eclecticism (as we currently use the word) does occur in Acts 17:18a in a very picturesque (though derogatory) term that was used by some Athenian Epicurean and Stoic philosophers to speak deprecatingly of the apostle Paul.[2] I have translated the portion of the verse in *The Christian Counselor's New Testament:*

Then some of the Epicurean and stoic philosophers took him on. Some said, "What does this eclectic babbler want to say?"

The Greek term that I have rendered "eclectic babbler" is *spermologos.* This word pictures birds picking up seed here and there. A bird does not stand in one place while feeding; it scurries about from place to place, often missing ground in between, pecking away first at this spot, then at that one. There seems to be no rhyme or reason, no method, no system to what it does. This hopping about from one idea to another, picking up scraps of information here and there to be pasted together in a senseless collage, of which the word *spermologos* speaks, aptly describes the opinion that those Athenians had of Paul. Because of the senseless patchwork quality of the results of such eclecticism, the Greek term in time also acquired the notion of babbling. To

---

1. For information, write: The Director, C.C.E.C., 1790 E. Willow Grove Ave., Laverock, PA 19118.
2. Ramsay says the word was a piece of Athenian slang.

preserve both nuances I translated it by the two words, "eclectic babbler."

Of course, the philosophers were wrong; Paul was not a hopping eclectic. Unlike the many speckled birds perched in the towers of Christian institutions today, he had definite views that (as he himself put it) he didn't receive "from a human being" nor was he "taught" by human beings but rather "received as a revelation from Jesus Christ" (Gal. 1:12). In his yet unanswered book, *The Origin of Paul's Religion*, J. Gresham Machen has fully demonstrated the fact that Paul's contention stands. No one with an open mind can read Machen's unparalleled work and still think that Paul was an eclectic.

But it is interesting to note that it was the adherents to two well-defined schools of thought—though diametrically opposed to one another—that united in their disdain of eclecticism as mere seed-picking that leads to babbling. Yet, as Luke describes their own activities in verse 21 (". . . the Athenians . . . spent their time doing nothing else but discussing and listening to new ideas"), it sounds very much as though they were not altogether immune to eclecticism themselves."[3]

I spend time with this Athenian reaction to Paul's market-place preaching because in it there so clearly lies the biblical refutation of the notion that eclecticism is an acceptable stance. By mentioning this incident, Luke intends to point out how erroneous the early opinions of these Greek philosophers were about Paul. The statement of those who called him a babbling seed-picker was as inaccurate as those who thought at first that "he seems to be promulgating some foreign gods" (v. 18b). Luke parenthetically points out that they said this because Paul had been preaching "Jesus and the resurrection (*anastasis*)." Evidently the word *anastasis* (resurrection) at first had been taken by them to be the proper name for a god (note the plural: "some foreign gods"). Because of these differing opinions (v. 18), they asked Paul to address them before the council of the Areopagus to learn just exactly what it was that he had to say (vv. 19, 20). But when he delivered his message, they not only were cleared up on the meaning of *anastasis*

---

3. Of course, like the council that condemned Socrates, they may have had more of a heresy-hunting spirit; but, N.B., even heresy-hunters (in spite of all that they say) at times may be lured into their interest in heresy by what I can only describe as a sort of eclectic curiosity. This seems to be what Luke had in mind when he wrote v. 21.

(vv. 31, 32) but, by his tactful yet ringing call for repentance (vv. 30, 31), understood that he was no tolerant eclectic either.[4]

There is, then, no evidence that eclecticism is condoned in the Scriptures. Indeed, to the contrary, the thrust of the entire Bible is against it. There is one emphasis from fore to aft in the Bible that is pointed up in the question that ought to be put to every eclectic: "How long will you lean to both sides?" (I Kings 18:21, Berkeley).

Down the long corridors of history, both in biblical times and since, Satan has levelled two basic forms of attack against the church. James R. Graham, in his book, *The Divine Unfolding of God's Plan of Redemption*, has called them *murder* and *mixture*. While murder has been successful at times (cf. the Islamic devastation of the church in North Africa), in general it has been a failure. Instead, as Tertullian observed, the blood of the martyrs has been "the seed of the church." But the use of *mixture*—from the beginning in the garden when Satan's counsel was mingled with God's—has proven to be highly effective. And what is eclecticism (in counseling as well as in other areas) within the church if it is not the modern form of that strategy?

How subtly, how easily, has Satan introduced his ideas into Christ's church in this way! And, in doing so, he has even found it possible to induce believing teachers to assist him. By convincing them that the pursuit of eclecticism is valid—and especially by the use of the eureka method (by means of which biblical truth is mistakenly equated with eclectic borrowings[5])—he has enlisted them to cover his tracks. The warnings of II John (especially vv. 8-11) are appropriate:

8 Watch yourselves, that you don't lose that which you have worked for, but rather that you may receive a full reward.
9 Everybody who goes beyond, and doesn't remain in the teaching of Christ, doesn't have God. The one who remains in the teaching has both the Father and the Son.
10 If someone comes to you and doesn't bring this teaching, don't receive him into your home and don't say "greetings" to him.
11 I say this because the one who says "greetings" to him shares in his evil deeds.

---

4. Cf. my remarks on this address in *Audience Adaptation in the Sermons and Speeches of Paul*, chapter 6, pp. 25-34; for implications relevant to Christian counseling see *More than Redemption* (Phillipsburg, N.J.: Presbyterian and Reformed, 1979), pp. xii, xiii.
5. For details on the Eureka method, see my *Lectures on Counseling*, pp. 34ff.

Among the grave dangers of eclecticism, I should like to mention four:

1. Satan's teachings are palmed off to unsuspecting persons as God's truth. (I do not say that those who engage in eclectic counseling are aware that this is what they are doing; no, the prevailing situation is that it is unsuspecting persons who thus influence other unsuspecting persons.)

2. The inevitable failures of eclectic approaches, as a result, are attributed to God, thus creating doubt and weakening faith in His Word.

3. Counselors are led further and further away from the study and application of the Scriptures in counseling while they become more and more concerned about the acquisition and implementation of human opinions. Usually this takes place so gradually that those who are involved in the transition are largely unaware of what is happening.

4. The emphasis on eclecticism has tended to encourage the development of a cast of self-styled Christian "professionals" who have been usurping the place of the pastor, who is God's counseling professional (II Tim. 3:15-17); these "professionals" have hung out shingles and on their own have gone into counseling as a business in competition to the church. Professionalism results.

These dangers constitute just cause for the Christian to do all that he can to discourage any further development of this deplorable situation.

I have pointed out before that Freud, Rogers, Skinner and all other such thinking framers of counseling systems, are wise enough to reject eclecticism. They recognize that one cannot adopt methods and procedures that were built on presuppositions about man and his predicaments that are contrary to their own, and that were designed to effect results and achieve goals that they do not share. The incredible fact is that so few Christian leaders see this. Truly, "the sons of this age are more shrewd with people of their own kind than are the sons of light" (Luke 16:8).

I could, of course, cite innumerable instances of eclectic borrowings and demonstrate how each has weakened some aspect of the Christian enterprise, but to do so would extend this chapter too greatly, and would (for those who would appreciate it) be majoring on the obvious. Instead, I wish to conclude with a plea to do all you can in the near future to diminish the influence of eclecticism in counseling and to promote the spread of biblical counseling. I am of the conviction that the spirit and practice of eclecticism is *the* most serious problem that the church faces today. Until that spirit is exposed to all and rooted out, the weaknesses in the church (of which we are all only too well aware) will never be replaced by the strength and might that comes from a strict and loving adherence to God's powerful Word.

10

"CPs," "ACPs" and "SCPs" in Counseling

From time to time I have spoken of complicating or secondary problems (CPs). By these, I refer to difficulties growing out of the presentation, or primary, problem that so complicate the counselee's life that there is no way in which he can solve it without first reaching a solution to them, or that must be dealt with after solving a primary problem before the case can be closed.

The fisherman accidentally gets a knot in his monofilament line. In attempting to untie it he manages instead to put five more knots in the line. Trying to loosen these, he only adds eight more, and so on, until he is ready to cut the line. This is the condition in which a counselee may come to counseling. But when he does,

1. he may not mention any (or some) of the 13 additional knots; he may focus on the first knot as if it were still his only difficulty. It is the counselor's task, through a judicious use of sub-questions stemming largely from the second basic question on the PDI, "What have you done about it?" to uncover every knot;[1]
2. often the complicating problem (or problems) will be like knots further along the line. That is to say, in order to get back to the original knot, the counselee first must be helped to untie all those knots that are encountered on the way up the line to the original knot.

Keeping these two important principles in mind will aid immeasurably in reaching final solutions that can be attained in no other way. Rushing ahead to tackle a presentation problem right off may not be the most efficient way to proceed, and (indeed) may itself lead to new complications. Counselees

---

1. Cf. my discussion of the Personal Data Inventory (PDI) in *Update on Christian Counseling* (Phillipsburg, N.J.: Presbyterian and Reformed, 1979), vol. 1, pp. 41-56.

have enough problems already; they don't need new ones that are manufactured in the counseling room.

The Bible warns against the baneful effects of unresolved complicating problems. In II Corinthians 2, for example, we read of the repentance of the excommunicated member who had been involved in incest. Now that the difficulty had been resolved through repentance, the member needed to be reassimilated into the body. As a result of his sin, the painful punishment of excommunication (a complicating problem) had been inflicted on him (v. 6). This was proper, and led ultimately to his repentance. But until he had been forgiven and comforted and the body had reaffirmed its love to him (vv. 7, 8), he was still in danger. Repentance was not enough. The repentance led to a remorse (a complicating problem) that could be removed only by reassimilation into the body. That is why Paul warns, "so, instead of going on with that [the punishment of excommunication], you should rather forgive and comfort him so that he won't be overwhelmed by too much pain." Note Paul's concern not only about repentance (all *some* would care about today), but also about the resolution of the entire situation, with all its ramifications, including its secondary or complicating features. That is seen clearly in the reason appended: "so that he won't be overwhelmed." There was a real danger of this if the reassimilation in loving forgiveness did not occur.

In this case, mentioned in II Corinthians 2, the primary problem *could* be handled first (as a matter of fact, it *had* to be), so that, unlike the knots that must be undone before it could be reached, *it might easily have been overlooked* had Paul not been aware of it and alerted the congregation to the possibility.

Thus, we see, the complicating (or secondary) problem that grows out of the initial (or primary) one may need to be dealt with either before or after handling the problem from which it has come. The danger in cases where complicating problems must be solved first is the failure to recognize their presence, leading to failure to solve either the primary problem or these secondary ones. In such cases, sessions eventually bog down, often with neither counselor nor counselee ever knowing why. The danger in cases where the complicating problems must be solved after solving the initial problem (again) is the possibility of failure to recognize their existence. But, unlike the former situation, a problem has been solved—indeed, usually the presentation problem itself. The success in doing so makes it very easy for both counselor and counselee to ignore further difficulties. And yet, as Paul noted in his concern for the recent excommunicant, all the good of the former solution could be undone by a failure to follow up the consequences of the original problem.

Thus, we may speak of *antecedent complicating problems* (ACPs) and of *sequential complicating problems* (SCPs, such as the case referred to in II Cor. 2). Of course, both are sequential in the sense that they are both secondary problems that grow out of primary problems. But the word "complicating" serves to indicate that fact. Thus the terms *antecedent* and *sequential* refer not to the origin of the problem but to the point at which the counselor deals with the problem.

A biblical instance of an antecedent complicating problem (ACP) is found in Hebrews 5:11: "We have a lot to say about this [the primary problem: to inform the reader about more advanced matters that they needed to know in order to live properly] but it is hard to explain since you have become dull in hearing [the ACP]."

Sometimes the complicating problem itself can grow as large as or greater than the original problem; *primary* and *secondary*, then, refer not to the significance or intensity of the problem, but to the question of which problem was occasioned by which. The situation in Corinth, in which several sins were being committed by some persons with reference to the Lord's supper, is a case in point. The sins of greed and drunkenness were serious, but the divine judgments that they occasioned (weakness, sickness and death[2]) became an *immediately* greater difficulty. Paul's message, therefore, was: judge yourself before the Lord does. Such circumstances demonstrate the *urgency* of dealing with primary problems immediately. Unless they are resolved quickly, they will lead to serious (or even irreparable) harm. The case here in Corinth clearly was a sequential complicating problem (SCP).

But in some SCP situations it is necessary to deal with the complicating

---

2. Cf. I Cor. 11:30ff.

79

problem right away. Someone who develops a bleeding ulcer due to worry and bitterness must first treat the ulcer (the SCP) or he may not live to deal with the primary problem (his attitude toward persons and life). The story of Cain in Genesis 4:3-12 involves a warning that God gave of the *possibility* of great complicating problems that would follow any failure to handle another problem immediately.[3] For your own interest, study II John 10, 11 and III John 9 to discover what kinds of complicating problems are mentioned and what must be done about them.

In conclusion, let me note several areas in which complicating problems frequently crop up for Christian counselors.

1. When a counselee has little or no hope, but is depressed, discouraged or in despair, you are faced with an ACP. Until you give him hope (or, perhaps it would be better to say, until hope has been generated within him) often there is no reason to expect that you can help him deal successfully with the difficulties over which he lost hope (cf. the section on hope in the *Manual*).

2. When a communication breakdown between two or more persons occurs as the result of failure to solve other problems (a *very* common phenomenon), what I have called the "communication dilemma" develops. That dilemma is this: to solve the interpersonal problems, including the communication problem, one must be able to communicate. I have shown how to overcome the dilemma in my book, *Christian Living in the Home*,[4] in the chapter on communication. But for now, let me simply observe that the communication breakdown is a striking instance of an ACP.

3. Closely related to the previous point (or as a part of it), the presence of anger, bitterness, mistrust, etc., results in an ACP. The problem here is that the *issue* in question cannot be dealt with until the *relationships* have first been set right. Nasty people, untrusting persons don't deal with issues properly.

Anger, frequently, is secondary to other feelings (such as disappointment, frustration or even fear). A parent may be very worried about the safety of a child who does not come home on time. But when he does show up, fear and worry change to anger. This dynamic must be recognized.

---

3. Cain's downcast attitude was itself a complicating problem growing out of his previous failure to bring a proper sacrifice. But unless *both* knots were unfastened, more would follow.
4. *Christian Living in the Home* (Phillipsburg, N.J.: Presbyterian and Reformed, 1972).

4. The paralyzing or fleeing effects of fear often lead to strong ACPs. The only force greater than fear is love (cf. my pamphlet on fear).

5. Sleep loss, when it leads to a state of easy irritation, inability to persevere in solving other primary problems, or even to perceptual difficulties (as it may in some cases), clearly presents you, as a counselor, with an ACP.

6. Life-dominating problems (LDPs, on which see the *Christian Counselor's Manual*) also give rise to both ACPs and SCPs. Here, in order to overcome the LDP, and a mopping up operation designed to insure against future failure of the same sort, through radical amputation and rehabilitation (see *More than Redemption*, chaps. 10, 16), you must deal with all sorts of other problems around the entire circle of the counselee's life pie that are tied into the LDP. It is not sufficient to focus on the LDP alone. LDPs, like drug addiction, drunkenness, homosexuality, etc., require total restructuring both *as the means* of breaking down the LDP and as a way of guarding against its recurrence.

7. Bad teaching, poor counsel, faulty attempts at solving primary problems also frequently end up producing a number of ACPs.

8. Organic illnesses, divine judgments, etc., may provide occasions for both ACPs and SCPs.

9. In general, it may be said that SCPs grow out of *consequences*. Loss of friends, jobs (and other sorts of losses) are a good example of this phenomenon. *In all cases* when you have reached a solution to a primary problem (and even when along with this some complicating problems have been resolved—particularly if they were ACPs), the question to ask is, "What have been the consequences of this problem?" A check list of these may reveal the necessity for further counseling. N.B., any given case may have one or more primary problems, to each of which may be attached both ACPs and SCPs.

It is my hope that this discussion will be enlightening to counselors who have not thought through the dynamics involved. The problem of CPs is so much a part of everyday counseling that we must all become aware of its presence.